ic Hirst
of Texas

Patrick E. Hopkins
Indiana University

Earnings: Measurement, Disclosure, and the Impact on Equity Valuation

**The Research Foundation of AIMR
and Blackwell Series in Finance**

Research Foundation Publications

Earnings: Measurement, Disclosure, and the Impact on Equity Valuation

To obtain the *AIMR Publications Catalog,* contact:
AIMR, 560 Ray C. Hunt Drive, Charlottesville, Virginia 22903, U.S.A.
Phone 804-951-5499; Fax 804-951-5262; E-mail info@aimr.org
or
visit AIMR's World Wide Web site at www.aimr.org
to view the AIMR publications list.

THE RESEARCH FOUNDATION OF THE ASSOCIATION FOR INVESTMENT MANAGEMENT AND RESEARCH™, THE RESEARCH FOUNDATION OF AIMR™, and THE RESEARCH FOUNDATION logo are trademarks owned by the Research Foundation of the Association for Investment Management and Research. CFA®, CHARTERED FINANCIAL ANALYST™, AIMR-PPS™, and GIPS™ are just a few of the trademarks owned by the Association for Investment Management and Research. To view a list of the Association for Investment Management and Research's trademarks and a Guide for the Use of AIMR's Marks, please visit our Web site at www.aimr.org.

© 2000 The Research Foundation of the Association for Investment Management and Research

All rights reserved. No part of this publication may be reproduced, stored in a retrieval system, or transmitted, in any form or by any means, electronic, mechanical, photocopying, recording, or otherwise, without the prior written permission of the copyright holder.

This publication is designed to provide accurate and authoritative information in regard to the subject matter covered. It is sold with the understanding that the publisher is not engaged in rendering legal, accounting, or other professional service. If legal advice or other expert assistance is required, the services of a competent professional should be sought.

ISBN 0-943205-49-2

Printed in the United States of America

August 2000

Editorial Staff
Roger S. Mitchell
Editor

Lisa S. Medders
Assistant Editor

Jaynee M. Dudley
Production Manager

Cheryl L. Likness
Production Coordinator

Lois A. Carrier
Composition

Mission

The Research Foundation's mission is to identify, fund, and publish research that is relevant to the AIMR Global Body of Knowledge and useful for AIMR member investment practitioners and investors.

Biographies

D. Eric Hirst is associate professor of accounting at the McCombs School of Business at the University of Texas at Austin, where he teaches courses in financial accounting and financial statement analysis in the MBA and Executive MBA programs. His current research focuses on individual investor judgment and decision making. Prior to Professor Hirst's academic career, he worked as a public accountant for KMG–Thorne Riddell in Toronto. In addition to receiving various research grants and awards for excellence in teaching and research, he is the author of papers published in the *Journal of Accounting Research*, *Contemporary Accounting Research*, the *International Tax Journal*, and other scholarly publications. Professor Hirst also serves as an *ad hoc* reviewer for the *Journal of Accounting Research* and *Accounting Horizons*. He is on the editorial board of the *Accounting Review*, *Auditing: A Journal of Practice & Theory*, and *Behavioral Research in Accounting*. He is associate editor of *Contemporary Accounting Research* and is a member of the American Accounting Association and the Canadian Academic Accounting Association. Professor Hirst holds a Ph.D. in accounting from the University of Minnesota.

Patrick E. Hopkins is an assistant professor and the OLIVE LLP Faculty Fellow at the Kelley School of Business at Indiana University, where he teaches advanced financial accounting topics. His research primarily investigates financial analysts' judgment and decision making in business and accounting settings. Prior to Professor Hopkins' academic career, he was a senior consultant with the public accounting firm Deloitte Haskins and Sells. In addition to receiving various research grants and awards for excellence in teaching and research, he is the author of papers published in the *Accounting Review*, the *Journal of Accounting Research*, and *Issues in Accounting Education*. He is on the editorial and advisory review board of the *Accounting Review*, and he has served as an *ad hoc* reviewer for numerous accounting and auditing journals. Professor Hopkins is a CPA and is a member of the American Institute of Certified Public Accountants, the American Accounting Association, and the Society for Judgment and Decision Making. He holds a Ph.D. from the Graduate School of Business at the University of Texas at Austin.

Contents

Foreword

It has long been accepted that the central function of security analysis is to forecast future accounting earnings for the purpose of valuation. Recent valuations, however, especially in the technology sector, have raised doubts in the minds of many investors as to the relevance of accounting earnings. Some analysts advocate the use of free cash flows in lieu of earnings. D. Eric Hirst and Patrick E. Hopkins tackle this crucial issue and provide persuasive evidence of the continued relevance of accounting earnings for the determination of investment value.

In addition to documenting the critical relationship between accounting earnings and security prices, Hirst and Hopkins offer a comprehensive compendium of earnings classifications to help analysts distinguish between transitory earnings and those earnings that are more likely to persist and thus affect future valuations. Hirst and Hopkins use a variety of real-world examples to illustrate these earnings classifications and to show analysts how to interpret them for the purpose of fundamental analysis.

Hirst and Hopkins next present the results of two original, controlled experiments to evaluate the use of accounting earnings by buy-side analysts. The first experiment reveals that analysts are often misled by opportunistic earnings management and, therefore, should focus greater attention on the sources and quality of earnings. The follow-up experiment shows that more comprehensive disclosure of the components of earnings helps to mitigate the problem of opportunistic earnings management and thus improves analysts' assessments of investment value. This latter finding strongly suggests that our profession should encourage policymakers to require greater transparency with respect to reported earnings.

This monograph is essential for anyone engaged in security analysis, whether a seasoned expert or a novice. Moreover, all investment professionals who seek a clear and thorough explication of accounting earnings and their relationship to valuation will benefit from the work of Hirst and Hopkins. The Research Foundation is pleased to present *Earnings: Measurement, Disclosure, and the Impact on Equity Valuation*.

Mark Kritzman, CFA
Research Director
The Research Foundation of the
Association for Investment Management and Research

©2000, The Research Foundation of AIMR

Acknowledgments

We thank the Research Foundation of AIMR for the opportunity to write this monograph and Keith Brown for his support of the project. We also received helpful feedback from our colleagues at the University of Texas at Austin and Indiana University—especially Daniel Beneish, Michael Clement, Roger Martin, Bob Parrino, Curt Rogers, and Jim Wahlen. We received comments on various parts of the project from workshop participants at Cornell University, the University of Florida, the University of Illinois, Indiana University, Ohio State University, the University of Utah, and Virginia Tech. The participants at the IU-NDU-PU Summer Research Conference, the Eighth Annual Conference on Financial Economics and Accounting, the University of Texas Summer Brownbag Workshop, the Financial Accounting Standards Board Professional Development Session, the 1998 Midwest AAA meeting, the 1998 Behavioral Decision Research in Management Conference, the 1998 American Accounting Association Annual Meeting, and the 1998 *Journal of Accounting Research* Conference also provided valuable comments. Lynette Wood provided research assistance.

We owe special thanks to Jeff Lucado, Walter Koon, Thomas Pence, and Gary Stratten for their efforts in helping us develop and administer the experiment reported in Chapter 3. In addition, we are indebted to the professional analysts and portfolio managers who unselfishly and anonymously donated their time to complete the case materials.

The usual caveats apply. Foremost among them is that we are solely responsible for any errors or omissions.

Dedication

The fact that you are holding a copy of this monograph is testament to the support and encouragement we have received from our families. We dedicate this work to them.

To

Patty, Kevin, and Matthew

Laura, Maggie, and William

Thanks!

©2000, The Research Foundation of AIMR

Introduction

Many textbook explanations of equity security valuation provide students and analysts with clear and concise explanations that give a false impression of the practical complexity of the valuation exercise. Part art and part science, part dissecting the past and part predicting the future—valuation is simultaneously a rewarding and frustrating process. On the one hand, gathering relevant information from a variety of sources and distilling it into a range of reasonable equity values is rewarding. It is the cornerstone of many individual and institutional investors' decisions to buy, sell, or hold securities. On the other hand, valuation is frustrating because it is fraught with uncertainty. First is the uncertainty associated with the exercise itself (for example, what is the right valuation model to use? Is the price too high? When will the market share my beliefs about the future and correct the price?). In addition, analysts find themselves playing cat-and-mouse games with the preparers of corporate financial statements. That analysts cannot simply take information reported in financial statements at face value is an aspect of equity valuation that significantly increases the complexity of an already difficult activity.

The rules that guide the preparation of financial statements in the United States (generally accepted accounting principles, or GAAP) allow company managers sufficient latitude to effectively communicate the financial position and results of the company operations. That same flexibility, however, also provides managers with the opportunity to conceal information from competitors, analysts, and other readers of the financial statements. In theory, when managers make financial reporting decisions, they trade off the potential benefits (e.g., reducing the cost of capital because disclosure reduces uncertainty) against potential costs (e.g., revealing proprietary information to existing and potential competitors). In addition, managers recognize that financial statements and their components affect contracts, including compensation contracts. Thus, managers may have significant incentives to paint a self-serving picture of the company. Prudent analysts, wary of the claims made in the financial statements, consider the source and context of the claims.

The goal of this monograph is simple: We want to increase analysts' understanding of how income statements and other disclosures can be used to assess the underlying quality and persistence of companies' economic activities. We believe the recent rush to "cash earnings" valuation models is caused by the need to justify sky-high prices for so-called new-economy stocks and is an overreaction to perceived weaknesses in the measurement of GAAP earnings. In the long run, however, cash earnings are unlikely to be the panacea that some claim they are.[1] Accounting data provide a rich source of insights into the intrinsic value of a firm. Harnessing the power of such information requires an understanding of its strengths and weaknesses. We hope that with the right tools and a thorough understanding of the inputs required to use them, security analysts will be able to generate accurate and insightful valuations of equity securities.

The monograph is organized as follows. In Chapter 1, we provide a brief review of the large body of research that explores the relationship between financial accounting information and security valuation. Although we deal only with selected research highlights, a clear picture emerges: Accounting data—in particular, reported earnings—are strongly related to security prices. We suggest that those who criticize financial accounting data as irrelevant are standing on shaky ground. We also review the claims that "cash is king" and accounting earnings are "a fiction," and we show that empirical results strongly support the relevance of accrual-basis accounting information.

In Chapter 2, we examine the question: What are earnings? We start with an overview of a powerful accounting-based valuation model. We also describe how accountants classify earnings into recurring and nonrecurring components. Then, we illustrate those classifications with actual disclosures and discuss how managers' judgments can lead to self-serving reporting. Armed with a good understanding of a company's accounting and its underlying strengths and weaknesses, the diligent analyst is in a good position to assess past performance. This understanding should lead to improved forecasts of future results.

Chapter 3 provides the results of two new empirical studies in which more than 100 members of the professional analyst community participated. The purpose of this discussion is to illustrate the difficulty underlying fundamental analysis and equity valuation. Our findings reveal that, in contrast to popular belief, the manner in which accounting data are reported predictably affects analysts' valuation judgments.

In Chapter 4, we close the monograph with a brief summary of our argument.

---

[1]The adage that "you manage what you measure" applies to cash earnings and cash flows as much as it does to accounting net income. Managing cash flow is as simple as delaying the payment of a supplier or running an advertising campaign a week earlier or later.

                                    ©2000, The Research Foundation of AIMR

Chapter 1. Evidence on the Relevance of Earnings to Valuation

In this chapter, we consider the empirical evidence for three aspects of the relevance of accounting earnings to valuation: the relationship between earnings data and stock prices, the information content of earnings data relative to the information content of cash flow data, and the use analysts make of earnings data in valuation.

In truth, a formal study of the role of accounting earnings in the capital markets is not needed to gauge the importance of reported income in the work of managers, analysts, and investors. Articles in the business press clearly focus significant attention on companies' quarterly and annual earnings announcements. Furthermore, corporate managers go to great lengths to explain the factors that influence reported income numbers and, increasingly, try to manage analysts' earnings expectations. For example, in recent years, the incidence of managers "talking down" investors' earnings expectations in the weeks leading up to an earnings announcement has increased. Their methods include initiating "whisper forecasts" and "preannouncing" earnings. In addition, the business press regularly provides comprehensive analyses of corporate valuations in terms of earnings-based multiples (e.g., the price-to-earnings ratio). Even articles announcing quarterly results for Internet companies include numerous adjustments and qualifications intended to guide the investing public to some estimate of (distant) future earnings.

The anecdotal evidence on the relevance of accounting earnings in security valuation may be interesting, but explicit conclusions about the relevance of earnings versus cash flows in valuation are best determined by observing the relationship between these metrics and stock prices. Fortunately, scholars in accounting and finance have conducted many studies of the relevance of accounting information for explaining the price levels and price changes of equity securities.

The following discussion briefly describes some of the classic research studies that demonstrate the relevance of accounting earnings for the purpose of equity security valuation.[1] Then, we consider studies that directly compare the relative usefulness of earnings and cash flows in valuation activities, although much of this discussion is at the level of market-determined stock prices. We conclude the chapter by describing results from the limited number of studies that have investigated how financial analysts actually use earnings-related information in valuation activities. This discussion provides the context for the experiment, described in Chapter 3, that investigates the effect of earnings on buy-side analysts' stock-price judgments.

Earnings Information and Equity Prices

For more than three decades, accounting and finance researchers have been rigorously investigating the relationship between accounting earnings and security prices. The relevance of this research lies not in allowing students or practitioners to pick winners before the fact but in its ability to explain variations in past stock prices. The fundamental question addressed in this research is whether, and to what extent, historical earnings are correlated with stock returns and/or stock prices. If *historical* earnings information is shown to be relevant in explaining current stock prices, then a valuation model that explicitly incorporates expectations of *future* earnings, such as the model we provide in Chapter 2, should be seriously considered by anyone practicing fundamental analysis.

Unexpected Earnings and Stock-Price Changes. A study by Ball and Brown (1968) provided the initial evidence that accounting earnings convey relevant information about the underlying value of securities. Their study laid the groundwork for much of the earnings-related academic research in accounting and finance that followed. Ball and Brown addressed the specific question of whether positive unexpected earnings are associated with positive changes in stock prices and whether negative unexpected earnings are associated with negative changes in stock prices. Although information from many sources is impounded in security prices, Ball and Brown isolated the effect of earnings on prices by looking at cross-sectional changes in earnings and the corresponding changes in prices. This design reduced the possibility that some factor other than the information aggregated in earnings was explaining stock-price changes.

---

[1]Although finance and accounting researchers have performed innumerable studies modeling and testing the relationship between earnings and stock returns and between earnings and stock values, the discussion in this chapter focuses on the most important lessons to be learned from a handful of the studies. For a more complete synthesis of research investigating the value relevance of earnings and other types of accounting information, see Bernard (1989), Lev (1989), Lev and Ohlson (1982), and Bauman (1996).

©2000, The Research Foundation of AIMR

Ball and Brown analyzed the net income and stock prices of 261 public companies between 1946 and 1966. Because the market should already have impounded the *expected* portion of these companies' earnings into stock prices, they hypothesized that the *unexpected* portion would predict stock-price change during the year for each of these companies.[2] They divided their sample into two groups—those with positive unexpected earnings and those with negative unexpected earnings. Their findings offer powerful support for the relevance of earnings. Specifically, having advance knowledge that a company will have a positive earnings change yields, on average, a 7 percent market-adjusted return on that stock. Likewise, having advance knowledge that a company will have a negative earnings change yields, on average, a 9 percent negative market-adjusted return on that stock.

Magnitude of Unexpected Earnings and Stock-Price Changes. Beaver, Clark, and Wright (1979) extended the work of Ball and Brown beyond investigating the *direction* of earnings changes to also examine the *magnitude* of earnings changes. Beaver et al. analyzed the net income and stock prices of 276 public companies between 1960 and 1975. They split the sample into 25 portfolios based on the ranked magnitude of the percentage change in residual (i.e., unexpected) net income for each company in each sample year. The final sample included approximately 106 company-years in each portfolio.

Table 1 provides the average residual change in earnings and the average residual change in price for the bottom five and top five portfolios composed in Beaver et al.[3] Portfolio 1 was the portfolio of stocks with the largest single-year decline (i.e., –154.8 percent) in unexpected earnings; Portfolio 10 was the portfolio of stocks with the largest single-year increase (i.e., 185.1 percent) in unexpected earnings. Note that Portfolios 1–5 lost more than 10 percent of their value in the year of the large negative earnings surprises whereas Portfolios 6–10 gained more than 10 percent of their value in the year of the large positive earnings surprises. Furthermore, evaluating the magnitudes of earnings surprises revealed much more pronounced return patterns than those observed in Ball and Brown. That is, the largest

---

2Ball and Brown used three proxies for unexpected earnings, with similar results for each. We limit our discussion to the random walk change in earnings or, more simply, the change in earnings from one year to the next. Ball and Brown also analyzed the abnormal returns on each company's stock. "Abnormal return" was defined as a company's common stock return for a month adjusted for the expected return as predicted by the capital asset pricing model (CAPM).

3The residual change in earnings measure used in Beaver et al. was a proxy for companies' unexpected earnings, and the residual change in price represents companies' common stock return for a month adjusted for the expected return as suggested by the CAPM.

Table 1. Average Residual Change in Earnings per Share and in Price for Bottom Five and Top Five Portfolios, 1960–75

Portfolio	Observations	Residual Change in EPS	Residual Change in Stock Price
1	107	−154.78%	−17.51%
2	107	−44.69	−12.40
3	106	−31.23	−14.69
4	106	−22.92	−11.76
5	106	−17.47	−11.33
6	106	28.70	10.44
7	106	36.28	11.79
8	106	49.72	15.76
9	106	72.06	22.23
10	106	185.08	29.16

Source: Adapted from Table 3 of Beaver et al. (1979).

negative stock return was −17.5 percent (compared with −9.0 percent in Ball and Brown), and the highest positive stock return was 29.2 percent (compared with 7.0 percent in Ball and Brown).

The asymmetric reaction to positive (29.2 percent) and negative (−17.5 percent) earnings surprises documented in Beaver et al. raises the possibility that the magnitude of a stock-price reaction may not be uniform for all levels or sources of earnings. These asymmetric results are not surprising in the context of our discussion in Chapter 2 about the varying sources and persistence of items that contribute to net income. Indeed, given companies' incentives to write off future expenses in a year that is already experiencing a net loss (i.e., to "take a bath"), the Beaver et al. relative stock-price return results for the highest and lowest portfolios of unexpected earnings are quite intuitive.

Determinants of Price Reaction. Although the pattern of results reported in Beaver et al. is consistent with intuition, these authors did not address the important issue of exactly what determines the magnitude of the stock-price reaction to a given level of unexpected historical earnings. This reaction, often referred to as the "earnings response coefficient" (ERC), is basically the slope coefficient between unexpected earnings and unexpected stock returns. For example, if a company was expected to report net income of $2 per share but actually reported net income of $3 per share, the unexpected earnings would equal $1. If the company's stock price increased by $5 per share based on this earnings announcement, the ERC would be 5. If all unexpected earnings were created equal, consistent ERCs would be observed, at least at the company level. But intuition suggests that some unexpected earnings are recurring and others are one-time events.

Kormendi and Lipe (1987) were the first to investigate whether ERCs can be explained by the extent to which one period's unexpected earnings become *expected* in the future.[4] That is, they believed the magnitude of companies' ERCs are (at least partly) explained by the portion of the earnings surprise that is expected to become part of normal earnings in the future. They found that, indeed, higher ERCs are associated with higher levels of future earnings *persistence*. In other words, stock prices respond the most to earnings changes that are indicative of future earnings performance.

Although a number of factors have been identified that affect the relationship between unexpected earnings and stock returns, the findings of Kormendi and Lipe and subsequent researchers indicate that this relationship depends in part on the extent to which earnings are expected to persist in the future. These results suggest that analysts should carefully consider the source and expected duration of earnings components when they include earnings in a valuation model.

Long-Term Relationships. Although Ball and Brown and Beaver et al. provided evidence that accounting earnings are relevant in pricing equity securities, the findings correlating earnings with stock prices or stock returns have suffered from low explanatory power. Models that correlate unexpected returns with unexpected earnings (aggregated over periods up to a year) rarely obtain R^2s in excess of 10 percent.[5] The implication is that the majority of stock returns over short time intervals are explained by factors other than one year's earnings. Easton, Harris, and Ohlson (1992) addressed this problem by analyzing the relationship between earnings and returns over a longer time period.

Easton et al. made two important contributions to the understanding of the earnings–stock returns relationship. First, they noted that the explanatory power of earnings should increase over longer return intervals because earnings aggregate over time and, therefore, the noise induced by possible income shifting and the noncomparability caused by the use of alternative

---

[4]The publication of this paper by Kormendi and Lipe spawned intensive investigation of ERCs by accounting researchers. An extensive review of ERC research can be found in Cho and Jung (1991).

[5]Loosely speaking, R^2 is the portion of variation in one variable that can be explained by the variation in another variable. Two variables that are perfectly correlated will have an R^2 of 1.0 (or 100 percent), and two variables that are randomly associated will have an R^2 of 0.

accounting methods should diminish over time. That is, over a long period, the various alternatives allowed by accrual accounting generally result in the same overall levels of aggregate accounting earnings. Second, they found that a long window allows investigation of the relationship between stock returns and the *aggregate* amount of earnings during the period. Most earnings research (for example, Ball and Brown; Beaver et al.) has generally investigated the correlation between unexpected earnings (or changes in earnings) and stock returns over short time frames.

Easton et al. analyzed the correlation between returns and earnings for 20 years of data from the 1987 Compustat data file.[6] They found that models correlating stock returns and the aggregate level of earnings over a 10-year period result in R^2s higher than 60 percent—a significant improvement in explanatory power over studies using short windows. In addition, their results pointed to the long-run relevance of accounting earnings in explaining the returns on common stock. The value relevance of long windows of aggregated historical earnings suggests that forecasting expected long-term future earnings should be useful for valuation purposes and even points to the potential usefulness in valuation of forecasting a company's net book value.[7]

Has the Value Relevance of Earnings Declined in Recent Years?
Although Easton et al. suggested that long-window earnings explain a large proportion of stock returns, many academics and analysts complain that quarterly and annual accounting earnings have become increasingly less relevant in explaining common stock returns. For example, many complain that the recurring reporting by companies of supposedly one-time items has recently increased. Elliott and Hanna (1996) confirm that reports of large, one-time items increased during the 20 years ending in 1994, and in particular, reports of large negative write-offs increased dramatically.[8] For example, in 1975, less than 5 percent of companies reported a large negative write-off, compared with 21 percent of companies in 1994. Elliott and Hanna also showed that the companies most likely to record these write-offs are companies that previously

---

[6]Their sample 20 years of data allowed the formation of ten 10-consecutive-year earnings samples. Each 10-year sample contained, on average, 1,045 companies.

[7]Net book value is equal to a company's assets minus its liabilities (i.e., it is equal to total owners' equity). Except when owners are investing or withdrawing capital, the net book value of a company changes as a result of earnings. Therefore, net book value is a metric that includes the historical aggregation of earnings of a company. Brennan (1995) noted that "the accretion to book value caused by the retention of earnings is eventually reflected in the stock price. Far from being close to useless, as some have claimed, accounting earnings are seen to be highly informative about stock returns over long time intervals" (p. 51).

[8]Elliott and Hanna defined large write-offs as those exceeding 1 percent of total assets.

©2000, The Research Foundation of AIMR

reported a similar write-off. The authors demonstrated that analysts' sarcasm about "recurring nonrecurring items" in quarterly and annual reports is justified. Their results point to a potential decline in usefulness of periodically reported bottom-line net income in the valuation of companies.

Collins, Maydew, and Weiss (1997) noted that factors leading to the decline in usefulness of single-period income measures might also lead to the increased relevance of net book value in valuing companies. To test this proposition, they analyzed the incremental explanatory power of net book value and earnings for stock prices for each of 40 years through 1993. They used a discounted abnormal earnings (DAE) valuation framework to investigate the relative importance of net book value and earnings. Briefly explained, DAE models suggest that the *total equity value* of a company can be expressed in terms of its future abnormal earnings and its current reported net book value.[9] From a valuation perspective, the important contribution of this framework lies in its ability to explain and predict stock values (i.e., prices) instead of changes in value (i.e., returns), which was investigated by much prior accounting research.

Collins et al. found that the average annual R^2s ranged between 0.5 and 0.75 when both earnings and book values were included in the valuation model. That is, together, earnings and net book value explained between 50 and 75 percent of the overall variation in stock prices—a substantial portion. In addition, consistent with the views of those who maintain that earnings have become increasingly less relevant, they found that the incremental explanatory power of bottom-line net income has indeed declined in the past 40 years. This finding reinforces the importance of evaluating the components of earnings rather than focusing on a single summary measure of profit. Collins et al. also found, however, that the incremental explanatory power of net book value has increased over the same period. To the surprise of those who argue that accounting has become less relevant to valuation, the total explanatory power of net income and net book value taken together has significantly increased in the past 40 years. In short, the Collins et al. findings are an important indicator of the relevance of accrual accounting information in explaining the levels of stock prices.

Taken together, these studies provide strong evidence that accrual-basis earnings information can be used to explain stock prices. Indeed, the results of these studies are so compelling that analysts would be wise to include an earnings-based model in their valuation repertoire.

---

[9]Chapter 2 contains a discussion of the DAE model.

The Information Content of Earnings versus Cash Flows

Chapter 3: Cash is King
—*Copeland, Koller, and Murrin (1996)*

Common sense tells us that accounting information is relevant for valuing stocks.
—*Brennan (1995)*

These quotations, each from eminent authors in finance, illustrate the perspectives in the finance community about the role of accrual accounting in equity valuation. The first perspective is based on the observation that the value of an asset is equal to the present value of its future cash flows. To determine a fair or intrinsic value for the bundles of cash flows embodied in an equity security, why not directly estimate those flows? From this perspective, an analyst logically begins the valuation process by evaluating current-period cash flows and then forecasting how they will change (or persist) in the future.

The perspective illustrated by the Brennan quotation is rooted in the observation that the financial reporting function is designed to provide information (i.e., earnings data) that summarizes the present and future net cash effects of the activities in which a company is engaged during a given period. From this perspective, one can rely on the accounting process to estimate and report the most likely cash flow implications of *operations* during the period. Furthermore, analysts can focus on the economic factors that influenced the company's core operating activities during the period and estimate the extent to which those factors will change or persist in the future. Indeed, as we note in Chapter 2, accountants classify income statements to aid in this endeavor.

In the previous section of this chapter, our discussion of the relevance of earnings in valuation did little to address the concerns of analysts, portfolio managers, and academics who believe that a company's cash flows, not earnings, are the only true indicator of a company's value. Although accounting earnings may be relevant to valuation, they say, these data are nonetheless inferior to direct measures of cash flow.

The reluctance of finance professionals to use reported earnings in valuation is usually because they believe companies have the ability to manage earnings data through the manipulation of accruals. This perspective, however, ignores an important fact that actually necessitates the preparation of financial statements on an accrual basis: Companies can also easily manipulate the timing of cash flows.

One of the important features of accrual-basis net income is that it is designed to quantify the expected effects on future cash flows of transactions and events that occur during a particular reporting period. Notwithstanding

©2000, The Research Foundation of AIMR

companies' ability to manage reported net income, accrual net income is a valuable starting point for determining the total present *and* future cash effects of the activities in which the company was engaged during the period, regardless of the timing of the receipt or disbursement of cash from those activities. Realized cash flow does not incorporate an expectation of the future and, therefore, may provide less useful information about the value of the company than accounting earnings. Furthermore, because accrual net income is linked to the underlying income-generating activity of the company, it provides a potentially more useful metric than cash flow for summarizing a company's creation of value during a period.

In a study directly comparing the relative informativeness of reported earnings and cash flows, Dechow (1994) evaluated the ability of companies' reported earnings and cash flows to explain stock returns for the 30 years ending in 1989.[10] She found that reported earnings are more strongly related to stock returns than are reported cash flows from operations or net cash flows for a given period. This association is even stronger for companies that are undergoing changes in their working capital needs or in their investing and financing activities.[11]

Sloan (1996) extended Dechow's analysis by plotting the ability of current earnings and free cash flows to predict future free cash flows. In his analysis, Sloan ranked companies' free cash flows (defined as operating cash flows plus investing cash flows) and net income. Each performance metric was divided by total assets to provide a more valid relative performance measure. He then ranked the companies on the basis of their relative free cash flow and earnings measures and generated portfolios of the highest and lowest 10 percent of the companies—that is, the top and bottom 10 percent of net income (NI) to assets and the top and bottom of free cash flow (FCF) to assets. Then, he observed the relative FCF performance for each portfolio for the succeeding five years. The high-current-NI portfolio consistently generated higher future FCFs than did the high-current-FCF portfolio. Similarly, the low-current-NI portfolio consistently generated lower future free cash flows than did the low-current-FCF portfolio.

---

[10]For a more in-depth explanation of the relative informativeness of earnings and cash flows, see Sloan (1996).

[11]On the other hand, one would expect cash flows to be more value relevant than accounting earnings in circumstances in which current earnings are not representative of future earnings. A study by Cheng, Liu, and Schaefer (1996) showed that cash flows explain more of stock returns when earnings are highly transitory (i.e., not permanent), which underscores the need to evaluate the components of earnings.

Interestingly, combined rankings of current-period earnings and cash flows appeared to provide the best measure of a company's ability to generate future free cash flows. As Sloan noted, the superiority of the combined performance measure suggests that overly aggressive accrual and deferral policies can hurt the predictive ability of earnings. By explicitly considering free cash flows, these aggressive accrual practices can be uncovered and explicitly considered. In other words, although current net income is a better predictor of future free cash flows than is current FCF, considering both measures simultaneously leads to even better predictions.

Sloan's findings suggest that analysts should use multiple valuation models in equity analysis. Specifically, his results provide evidence that analysts would be wise to first consider an earnings-based valuation model (such as a discounted abnormal earnings model) and qualify the inputs to that model by using a cash-flow-based analysis. His findings also support the importance of fundamental financial statement analysis in security analysis. Sloan's results are extraordinary in light of the coarseness of the measures he used to partition the companies. Additional in-depth analysis of earnings and cash flows should lead to even stronger results.

Analysts' Use of Earnings in Valuation

The research discussed so far has focused on the informativeness of cash flow and accrual accounting information in explaining market-determined stock prices. As for the importance of earnings in analysts' valuation activities, although abundant anecdotal evidence exists, researchers have little understanding of how analysts actually use this information or what features of earnings-related information have the most influence on analysts' valuation judgments.

A significant source of the demand for earnings-related information is the professional analyst community. Sell-side analysts require historical earnings information because forecasts of future earnings (in addition to valuation estimates and buy/hold/sell decisions) are an important output of their analysis activities. The accuracy of these forecasts can determine to a significant extent whether analysts are included on annual all-star lists and can, to a lesser extent, determine a portion of their variable compensation. Sell-side analysts' reports generally include detailed discussions of earnings and earnings components, but the link to valuation assessments is not well specified. Furthermore, evidence suggests that because sell-side reports are not independently derived predictions of the future and can be influenced by the underwriting relationship between the target company and the analyst's

©2000, The Research Foundation of AIMR

employer, the value of these reports is discounted by buy-side analysts and portfolio managers.[12]

For analyzing the role of earnings in valuation, buy-side analysts and portfolio managers would provide a much more independent source of information than sell-side analysts. And based on interviews with buy-side analysts reported in such publications as *Barron's*, earnings are relevant to many buy-side analysts. Buy-side analysts' activities, however, are generally considered proprietary. Therefore, researchers have not been able to directly observe the valuation-driven demand or use of earnings information by buy-side analysts. In addition, buy-side analysts have many competing demands for their time during a normal business day. Because contacting individual buy-side analysts is difficult and because these analysts have difficulty finding the time necessary to assist with academic research, only a handful of studies have investigated the role of earnings and other accounting information in valuation.[13]

Mear and Firth (1987, 1990) published a series of articles that addressed the role of earnings in buy-side analysts' valuation activities. The articles were based on a single experiment they conducted with 38 buy-side analysts and portfolio managers. They conducted the experiment by presenting each analyst with 30 similar short cases in which the authors varied nine pieces of company-specific information (e.g., company profitability, price-to-book value) and one piece of industry-specific information. Because each analyst considered all 30 cases, the information was in a highly summarized format.

In their 1987 article, Mear and Firth reported whether analysts have self-insight into the factors that affect their judgments of (1) the expected risk and (2) the 12-month expected return of an individual stock within a well-diversified portfolio. The authors found that earnings-related (i.e., profitability) information was the most important factor in their return judgments and the second most important factor in their risk judgments. Although the materials provided to analysts were highly simplified and the authors did not provide

---

[12] A number of studies analyzed sell-side analysts' reports. For example, in a sample of 479 sell-side analysts' reports, Previts, Bricker, Robinson, and Young (1994) noted that earnings-related information is the factor most cited by sell-side analysts. In a follow-up study, Bricker, Previts, Robinson, and Young (1995) investigated the factors that determine whether sell-side analysts believe companies have "high-quality" earnings.

[13] A number of studies conducted during the 1980s (e.g., Anderson 1988) analyzed the *pattern* of information use by small samples of analysts. These studies provided evidence on the styles of information searches conducted by professional analysts, but they generally did not address the relevance of specific pieces of accounting information (e.g., earnings) in analysts' valuation activities.

cash flow information, the findings suggest that earnings are an important input into the valuations made by buy-side analysts.

In their 1990 article, Mear and Firth found that after the analysts were grouped by investment style, earnings-related information continued to be an important input in stock-return judgments.

Summary

More than 30 years of academic research in accounting and finance has documented the relevance of accounting earnings for explaining both the levels of and changes in equity security prices. Recent research has demonstrated that, contrary to the position of those who argue that accrual accounting data are increasingly irrelevant, the combined explanatory power of earnings and book value has not declined in the past 40 years. Other results indicate that if one's goal is to estimate *future* free cash flows, current earnings do a better job than do current free cash flows. The combination of current earnings and current free cash flows predicts future free cash flows even better.

Finally, Mear and Firth provided important evidence about the relative use of earnings information in analysts' judgments. The design of their study, however, did not allow conclusions to be drawn about a number of valuation-related issues discussed in this monograph. In particular, Mear and Firth did not provide cash flow information to their analyst participants, so inferences about the relative importance of earnings versus cash flows could not be made. In addition, because they provided only summary measures of profitability, Mear and Firth could make no conclusions about analysts' abilities to use income statement information to assess the underlying quality of a given level of net income. The experiment we report in Chapter 3 was designed to address these important issues.

        ©2000, The Research Foundation of AIMR

Chapter 2. The Reporting of Earnings and Equity Valuation

IS NIKE BACK IN STYLE?. . . The Street seems to think so. Alex. Brown raised Nike to buy from market perform; Morgan Stanley upped it to a strong buy; Goldman upped it to market outperform. Why all the kisses? Well, Nike beat analyst estimates by a whole penny! Good dog! It's okay that earnings were 4 cents versus 52 cents last year, that revenues fell 3 percent, that worldwide futures orders were down 13 percent, and that there's no sign of renewed sneaker sales in Asia. Oh, yeah, and that earnings figure excludes a $130 million restructuring charge. Include it, and the company lost $67.7 million, its first loss in more than a decade. (But we all know restructuring isn't real money.) None of that matters, because Nike's stock costs only $52 versus $58 at this time last year. And everything else has gone up, so really, Nike's even cheaper! Haven't you heard of relative value??

—Serwer (1998)

We just want you to remember that accounting earnings are slippery animals . . . to be forewarned is to be forearmed.

—Brealey and Myers (1991)

In Chapter 1, we presented evidence on the association between accounting data and security prices and returns. This chapter begins with a brief discussion of a valuation model that is derived from the dividend discount model and uses accounting data as a direct input. The fundamental strength of this model is that it is consistent with traditional cash-based valuation but does not require analysts to forecast the timing of actual cash flows or worry about reversing the effects of future accruals from accounting information. From both a theoretical and a practical perspective, this accounting-based valuation model can serve as a primary instrument in analysts' equity valuation toolkits.

Regardless of the valuation model used, analysis of historical earnings is usually an important precursor to forecasting relevant inputs.[14] But what are the relevant historical earnings? Net income? Operating income? Income

---

[14]For example, in a common application of the free cash flow model, a company's current period earnings are used to forecast future years' earnings. Then, after forecasted future earnings are estimated, the analyst removes forecasted future noncash items from earnings to arrive at forecasted cash flows.

before extraordinary items? Comprehensive income? Of course, the definitive answer to the question is: It depends. As when using any information, what data are relevant depends on what one is trying to learn and what one wants to do with the answer. If, for example, an analyst needs to know earnings to compare that datum with a bond covenant or the terms of a compensation agreement, then the analyst needs to know the contract's definition of earnings. If the focus is on equity valuation, then the analyst probably wishes to evaluate management's past performance to help predict the company's future performance. To do so, the analyst will want to determine the components of earnings most likely to persist in the future and the components most likely not to recur. Unfortunately, no clear, single definition of earnings is relevant for this endeavor. However, if the analyst understands the basic income figures reported and the types of information that usually supplement the income figures, the analyst can make a clearer prediction of future income.

Following our discussion of earnings-based valuation, we outline the way accounting earnings in the United States are currently reported. We use the financial statements of a number of companies to illustrate our points. As the reader will see, not all items that affect earnings are included on the face of the income statement. In addition, some items that are probably not representative of future earnings are included in determining current-period net income. Our goal is to provide an overview of the various categories of income statement items so analysts can assess the underlying quality of reported net income.[15] Consistent with the opening quote from Brealey and Myers, we believe that a better understanding of accounting data will lead to better analyses.

Free Cash Flow Models or Earnings-Based Models?

It is best to remember that cash is a fact, earnings an opinion.

—Rappaport (1998)

The DCF [discounted cash flow] technique has the beguiling appeal that cash flows are "real," whereas accounting earnings are artifacts. But is DCF really worthy of enthronement? If it is king, then the king's subjects are poorly served.

—Penman (1992)

Although few would argue with the theoretical merits of cash-based models, such as the dividend discount model or the free cash flow (FCF) model, the

---

[15]We use the term "quality" to refer to the extent to which the current-period earnings are useful in predicting future earnings.

©2000, The Research Foundation of AIMR

preceding quotations illustrate a fundamental divergence of opinion about the use of earnings in everyday equity valuation. Our view, supported by a growing body of empirical research, is that earnings-based models, properly applied, are particularly useful tools for security analysts. Such models, derived directly from the dividend discount model, can be used to value securities. An earnings-based model's key strengths are the ease with which intuitive economic notions are incorporated into its inputs, its integration into models for comprehensive financial statement analysis (such as the DuPont model of return on equity), and the manner in which it reduces the "terminal value problem" associated with FCF models.

Some argue that FCF models are superior to earnings-based models because FCF models use the "true" flows that matter to shareholders—cash flows.[16] Accounting earnings, they argue, are subject to manipulation by management, suffer from a conservative bias in accounting standards, and sometimes omit important elements of economic income. Although most observers recognize that corporate managers time payments (and, to some degree, receipts) of cash to manage cash flows, the perception is that cash flows are real and accounting earnings are not.[17] For example, Copeland, Koller and Murrin (1996) claimed that, just as one cannot buy groceries with earnings (only with cash), analysts should use DCF methods, rather than earnings, to value a company. This argument hinges on the assumption that current cash flow (versus current earnings) is a better measure of future cash flow. Of course, this issue is an empirical one, and the research evidence

---

[16]We believe that the "cash is king" perspective is an extremist view, especially when considering the typical application of cash-flow models (including FCF models) in practice. In typical real-world applications, expected future FCF is generally derived by first forecasting future income statements and balance sheets. Furthermore, *historical* financial statements are the most common starting point for forecasting future financial statements. Reflecting on the sequence of steps in this estimation process quickly reveals that analysts apply FCF models by forecasting and analyzing the very data the models are designed to avoid—accrual accounting data. So, although forecasted accruals are unwound in the models to arrive at the free cash flows, the models are highly dependent on accounting-based measures of performance.

[17]Just as accounting-based earnings can be manipulated, so can cash flows—and the aggressive timing of cash flows is not likely to spark problems with the auditors! Consider a simple way to increase cash flow in the current period: Pay suppliers on the first day of the following period. Although it might be clear that the company is trying to make the current period's ending cash position look strong, no auditor would force the company to record the cash payment (from next period) in the current period. If the account payable arose because a service was consumed this year (and was likely to be consumed again next year), the auditor would surely require the company to include the related expense in determining the current period's earnings. Indeed, accrual accounting requires that the cost of currently consumed goods and services be included in determining a company's profitability.

reported in Chapter 1 suggests that the assumption is suspect. Indeed, research evidence points to current earnings as a superior predictor of future cash flows.

Given the potential benefits of an earnings-based valuation approach, the primary hurdle becomes identifying a rigorous and descriptively valid model. Fortunately, recent theoretical advances in accounting provide a valuation model that uses accounting data as a direct input.[18] Derivation of this model, called the discounted abnormal earnings (DAE) model, begins with two fundamental relationships. First,

$$B_t = B_{t-1} + E_t - D_t, \tag{1}$$

where
B_t = ending book value of equity
B_{t-1} = beginning book value of equity
E_t = current-period earnings
D_t = current-period dividends

Equation 1 is known as the "clean surplus relation." It says that ending book value of equity equals beginning book value plus current-period earnings less current-period dividends.[19]

The second fundamental relationship is

$$E_t = \text{ROE}_t \times B_{t-1}. \tag{2}$$

That is, current-period earnings can be expressed as the current-period return on equity (ROE_t) times the beginning book value of equity.

These relationships are not controversial. They simply draw on the fundamental accounting equation and basic notions of returns. A relationship between accounting data and equity valuation develops when the clean surplus relation is rearranged (solving for dividends) and substituted into the dividend discount model:

$$P_0 = \sum_{t=1}^{\infty} \frac{D_t}{(1+r)}, \tag{3}$$

---

[18] See, for example, Ohlson (1995), Feltham and Ohlson (1995), and Edwards and Bell (1961). Empirical support for the model as a predictor of value is available in, among others, Bernard (1995), Francis, Olsson, and Oswald (2000), and Penman and Sougiannis (1998).

[19] Two important points need to be clarified. First, earnings in Equation 1 are defined as clean surplus earnings. Technically, therefore, "comprehensive income" (not "net income") is the correct performance measure. (Comprehensive income is discussed in more detail later in this chapter.) Second, dividends are defined as dividends in the normal use of the term plus share repurchases less share issuances.

                                    ©2000, The Research Foundation of AIMR

where

P_0 = intrinsic value of the company's equity at time 0
D_t = expected dividends at time t
r = cost of equity capital

Equation 3 leads to

$$P_0 = \sum_{t=1}^{\infty} \frac{E_t - (B_t - B_{t-1})}{(1+r)^t}. \qquad (4)$$

This reformulation of the dividend discount model can be further rearranged to yield[20]

$$P_0 = B_0 + \sum_{t=1}^{\infty} \frac{E_t - rB_{t-1}}{(1+r)^t}$$

$$= B_0 + \sum_{t=1}^{\infty} \frac{\text{ROE}_t - rB_{t-1}}{(1+r)^t}. \qquad (5)$$

That is, the intrinsic value of a company's equity at time 0 equals the accounting book value of equity plus the sum of discounted future abnormal earnings, or earnings above the required rate of return on opening book value (i.e., $[\text{ROE}_t - r] \times B_{t-1}$).[21] Because the model focuses on returns to common equityholders, the appropriate discount rate is the cost of equity capital.

An important benefit of the DAE valuation technique is one of framing the valuation question. As is clear from Equation 5, the required inputs are not future dividends (i.e., value *distribution*) but rather the relationship between future earnings and future book value (i.e., value *creation*).

Another key feature of the model is the relationship between future abnormal earnings and the notion of competitive equilibrium. When competitive

---

[20]White, Sondhi, and Fried (1998) used the relationships in Equations 1 and 2, together with the fact that $B_t/(1+r) = B_t - rB_t/(1+r)$, to derive Equation 5. The process involves expanding Equation 4 for $t = 1$ and 2 and substituting the aforementioned relationship for $B_t/(1+r)$. After reducing the resulting equation for terms that cancel out and expanding from $t = 3$ to $t = \infty$, Equation 5 results.

[21]Note that economic value added (EVA) and DAE are both models of "residual income." That is, they both attempt to capture the value created by a company after providing returns to *all* providers of capital. Accounting earnings, through interest expense, consider the return to debtholders, but because accounting earnings do not include a charge for the cost of equity capital, they overstate residual income. By explicitly considering the equity capital invested to generate the returns, EVA and DAE capture measures of residual income. Using residual income to value entities can be traced to work by Preinreich (1938).

equilibrium is reached—and it is hard to imagine most companies not reaching that level in a relatively short time[22]—the company's *abnormal* earnings become zero (i.e., ROE = r) and are irrelevant to valuation. Thus, the forecasted terminal value term in the pragmatic versions of the dividend discount model and the FCF model is absent. The DAE model replaces it with a currently observable measure, namely, opening book value. Indeed, the terminal-value problem is completely eliminated if financial statement forecasts are made for the period in which the company is expected to reach competitive equilibrium.

To be sure, some companies will not reach competitive equilibrium in which abnormal earnings equal zero or will earn *accounting*-based ROE greater than the cost of equity capital. In the former scenario, the company may have established barriers to entry or competitive advantages that are indefinitely sustainable. In the latter case, conservative accounting may, in effect, overstate ROE. For example, U.S. pharmaceutical companies are required to immediately expense their research and development costs. When the R&D is expected to generate future profits, this requirement leads to an understatement of current equity. When those future profits arise, they will then be compared with an understated B_{t-1}, and the resulting ROE_t may appear to exceed the cost of equity capital. These "abnormal earnings" are more a function of accounting measurement error than of true economic excess profits. Note that if the book value of equity equaled the market value of equity, then in competitive equilibrium ROE would likely equal the cost of equity capital. Regardless of the book value–market value relationship, the DAE model generally reduces the magnitude of the terminal value problem and enhances the interpretation of the term.

Finally, the DAE model is explicit in the emphasis placed on ROE. In fact, forecasting abnormal future earnings hinges on the analyst's ability to forecast future ROE. Well-known ROE decompositions, such as DuPont analysis, allow the analyst to focus on *why* ROE will achieve a certain level and *why* its growth will (or will not) persist.[23] Thus, the valuation task is closely tied to the analyst's views of company operating profitability and efficiency, leverage, tax rates, and so on. This characteristic allows careful business analysis to be explicitly integrated into the valuation exercise.

How does a model that ignores cash flows in favor of accounting figures capture value? Accrual-based accounting earnings are designed to measure value creation. But everyone knows that some companies manage earnings

---

[22]Figure 3.1 in Palepu, Bernard, and Healy (1996) shows that most U.S. industrial companies earn 10–14 percent ROE and that abnormally high or low ROEs in a given year tend to revert to the 10–14 percent range within three years.

    ©2000, The Research Foundation of AIMR

and that accounting numbers may distort economic reality. Indeed, in applying economic value added (EVA)—a specific version of DAE—to value securities, Goldman, Sachs & Company (1997) indicates that some 160 adjustments to accounting data are required (although Goldman Sachs applies a much smaller subset). How does the DAE model capture these distortions? The answer lies in the complementary relationship between book value and abnormal earnings. **Exhibit 1** illustrates this relationship and provides a specific example of why different revenue-recognition methods do not affect overall DAE valuation.

An important constraint on this analysis is that analysts must consider the rules under which accounting data are generated. For example, if a company is recognizing revenue and earnings on an aggressive basis, Exhibit 1 illustrates that the DAE valuation will be unaffected *only if* the analyst properly estimates the drop in future abnormal earnings resulting from the early recognition of earnings. More generally, the method requires that analysts explicitly consider "accounting quality" and determine how the numbers reported in the past are likely to affect the figures reported in the future. If aggressive reporting leads the analyst to overestimate the amount of overall future abnormal earnings, the DAE model will not magically self-correct the valuation.[24]

---

[23] Although DuPont analysis comes in a variety of forms, one useful form breaks down ROE into NI/CSE = NI/EBT × EBT/EBIT × EBIT/Sales × Sales/Assets × Assets/CSE, where NI is net income, CSE is common shareholders' equity, EBT is earnings before taxes, and EBIT is earnings before interest and taxes. The first term in the breakdown of ROE measures the proportion of earnings retained after paying taxes (i.e., 1 – Average tax rate). The second term represents the proportion of earnings before interest and taxes that belongs to the equityholders. The third term is operating return on sales. The fourth term is total asset turnover, and the final term is a measure of leverage (i.e., Liabilities/CSE + 1). The model can be easily extended to incorporate comprehensive income (CI) into ROE by substituting CI for NI in return on equity and adding an additional term into the decomposition (CI/NI) that captures the after-tax effect on ROE for items of other comprehensive income.

[24] Consider the case of Sunbeam Corporation as described by Laing (1998). The company was accused of manufacturing its 1997 earnings through various aggressive accounting choices and by "preselling" products ahead of normal schedules. Preselling can come in many forms, including offering deep discounts to distributors at the end of a given quarter, offering very liberal return policies, and billing for goods that have not been shipped. Sunbeam is alleged to have paid some distributors a monthly fee to hold gas grills at the distributors' warehouses. In addition, particularly loose return policies applied to the goods. *Barron's* compared these sales to consignment sales (which normally would not be recorded as revenue). The DAE model would accommodate this accounting as long as the analyst recognized that past earnings may not be representative of future results. Aggressive year-end discounting and accounting lead to high current abnormal earnings, but via their effect on increased book value, the threshold level of earnings required to record future *abnormal* earnings is raised. Because the aggressive revenue recognition in prior periods means that those revenues will not be reported in later periods, the chance of high future abnormal earnings is lowered.

Exhibit 1. The Effect of Accounting Choice on DAE Valuation

Consider a company that has a book value of $1,000,000 at $t = 0$. During the next two years, the company will have total revenues of $5,000,000 and total net income of $220,000. All revenues are eventually collected and all costs are paid in cash by the end of the second year, which is when the company liquidates. Assume that the company's cost of equity capital is 10 percent.

We examine two scenarios. In the first, revenue and earnings are recognized equally over the two-year period. In the second, the company reports revenue aggressively in Year 1 at $4,000,000 and thus reports $176,000 of earnings. The following year, the company recognizes $1,000,000 of revenues together with the remaining $44,000 of earnings.

Scenario	Calculation	
Opening book value		$1,000,000
Scenario 1		
Year 1		
Abnormal earnings	$110,000 - (1,000,000 \times 10\%) = \$10,000$	
Discounted abnormal earnings	$\$10,000 \times 1.10^{-1}$	9,091
Year 2		
Abnormal earnings	$110,000 - (1,110,000 \times 10\%) = -\$1,000$	
Discounted abnormal earnings	$-\$1,000 \times 1.10^{-2}$	−826
Value of equity		$1,008,264
Scenario 2		
Year 1		
Abnormal earnings	$176,000 - (1,000,000 \times 10\%) = \$76,000$	
Discounted abnormal earnings	$\$76,000 \times 1.10^{-1}$	69,091
Year 2		
Abnormal earnings	$44,000 - (1,176,000 \times 10\%) = -\$73,600$	
Discounted abnormal earnings	$-\$73,600 \times 1.10^{-2}$	−60,826
Value of equity		$1,008,264

Note: Assume that at the end of Year 2, the company liquidates and thus pays a terminal dividend equal to book value, or $1,220,000. The present value of that dividend equals $1,220,000 (1.10^{-2}, or $1,008,264).

Accounting systems are simply sets of rules that relate economic events—some observable, some not—and financial statements. Although imperfect, accounting reports are designed to provide analysts with information useful for predicting future earnings and cash flows. Indeed, the accounting classifications we describe next have that purpose. Understanding what has been recorded in book value or in earnings (and why) helps analysts predict future patterns of earnings and book values—that is, the inputs to DAE valuation.

©2000, The Research Foundation of AIMR

The Classified Income Statement

In the United States, standards dealing with income statement classification have largely proceeded on a by-exception basis. For the most part, accounting standards use the all-inclusive approach, whereby all revenues and expenses and all gains and losses for a period are included in the period's income statement. Within that framework, standards have evolved for treating ordinary versus extraordinary items and continuing versus discontinued operations. These categories are designed to help readers of financial statements determine the origin and assess the persistence of the various earnings components.

Income statements generally include the following broad categories or line items:

Sales

Cost of goods sold
    Gross profit

Other operating revenues and expenses, including both
    recurring and nonrecurring items
        Operating income

Financing and other costs
    Pretax income from continuing operations

Income tax on continuing operations
    Income from continuing operations

Discontinued operations, net of tax (separated into results of
    operations and gain or loss on disposal)

Extraordinary items, net of tax

Cumulative effects of accounting changes, net of tax

Net income

Harnischfeger Industries' 1995 income statement provides a detailed example of these categories, as shown in **Table 2**.

Under a pure all-inclusive approach to reporting income, net income captures all changes in owners' equity except those involving transactions with owners. That is, net income and dividends are the items that reconcile opening and ending retained earnings as follows:

Assets – Liabilities = Owners' equity (i.e., Contributed capital
                    + Retained earnings).

Thus,

$\Delta A - \Delta L = \Delta$Contributed capital + ΔRetained earnings
    $= \Delta$Contributed capital + Net income – Dividends.

Table 2. Harnischfeger Industries Statements of Income
(dollar amounts in thousands, except per-share amounts)

	1995	1994	1993
Revenues			
Net sales	$2,152,079	$1,551,728	$1,409,204
Other income	61,865	23,301	9,040
Total revenues	$2,213,944	$1,575,029	$1,418,244
Cost of sales	1,671,932	1,195,851	1,083,846
Product development, selling, and administrative expenses	330,990	279,016	259,831
Restructuring charges	—	—	67,000
Nonrecurring charge	—	—	8,000
Operating income (loss)	211,022	100,162	(433)
Interest expense, net	(40,713)	(47,366)	(48,313)
Income (loss) before Joy[a] merger costs, provision (credit) for income taxes, and minority interest	$170,309	$52,796	($48,746)
Joy merger costs	(17,459)	—	—
Provision (credit) for income taxes (including credit of $6,075 relating to Joy merger costs)	53,500	13,979	(16,497)
Minority interest	(7,230)	(2,224)	4,799
Income (loss) from continuing operations (after deducting $11,384, net of applicable income taxes, related to Joy merger costs)	$92,120	$36,593	($27,450)
Income (loss) from and (net loss) on sale of discontinued operations, net of applicable income taxes	(31,235)	(3,982)	7,760
Extraordinary loss on retirement of debt, net of applicable income taxes	(3,481)	(4,827)	—
Cumulative effect of accounting change, net of applicable income taxes and minority interest	—	(81,696)	—
Net income (loss)	$ 57,404	($ 53,912)	($ 19,690)

Note: For years ended October 31.

[a]Joy Mining Machinery.

Source: Harnischfeger Industries 1995 annual report.

©2000, The Research Foundation of AIMR

In recent years, however, accounting standards have allowed a number of items to bypass the income statement, resulting in changes made directly to owners' equity (i.e., "dirty surplus"). Currently, the major items treated this way are certain foreign-currency-related items (under Statement of Financial Accounting Standards No. 52), certain financial-instrument-related items (under SFAS No. 80), certain pension-liability-related items (under SFAS No. 87), certain marketable-security-related items (under SFAS No. 115), and certain derivatives-related activities (under SFAS No. 133).

Since 1998, SFAS No. 130, *Reporting Comprehensive Income*, has required companies to report an income figure that incorporates net income and changes in these dirty surplus items. Because these additional items typically have low levels of persistence, they should not directly affect analysts' forecasts of future abnormal earnings. Comprehensive income can, however, include additional information relevant to valuations and should be considered part of diligent fundamental analysis. Thus, we begin our discussion of accounting analysis with the most important value-relevant data—income from continuing operations—and discuss comprehensive income in detail at the end of the chapter.

Income from Continuing Operations. Income from continuing operations, as the name implies, is the profit reported in the current period from the operations that management purportedly expects to continue in the future. It should not be interpreted as permanent or recurring earnings because companies systematically include items in it that reasonably can be expected to occur only once. Sometimes, the reason is restrictive accounting rules; sometimes, it results from "strategic reporting" on the part of the company managers. For example, a common belief is that managers are more likely to highlight one-time losses than one-time gains in communications with shareholders and in the business press.[25] So, analysts should always study the notes and other sources to develop an unbiased assessment of the company's recurring earnings stream. Some of the more common nonrecurring items are unusual items and restructuring charges.

---

[25]Schrand and Walther (2000) find that managers are more likely to remind investors about prior-period gains than losses. They argue that this practice is strategic in nature; that is, companies are attempting to manage perceptions of what a reasonable performance benchmark is. They find that in quarterly earnings announcements, managers tend to highlight prior gains on property, plant, and equipment dispositions to reduce the potential benchmark against which current earnings are evaluated. Managers do not highlight prior-period losses on disposal of the same items, which leads to an emphasis on the greatest possible improvement in quarter-over-quarter earnings. Reminding investors about prior gains serves to reduce the benchmark, and ignoring prior losses serves to keep the benchmark low.

Unusual and Nonrecurring Items.

> To be fair, IBM's policy of taking nonrecurring charges on a recurring basis does make estimates [of earnings] rather chancy and, indeed, gives a wonderfully surreal quality to its earnings, since the charges not only reconfigure the past but conceivably prefigure, by anticipating expenses, the future.
>
> *—Abelson (1996)*

Terms such as "discontinued operations" and "extraordinary items" are income statement classifications specifically defined in accounting standards, but the term "unusual items" is a catchall phrase referring to items that do not meet more specific definitions. Because "unusual items" do not have a restrictive definition, managers often describe an income statement item as "unusual" to draw readers' attention to it. In practice, these items are explicitly labeled "unusual" on the face of the income statement, or they are more fully described as such in the notes or in the management discussion and analysis.

For example, in the 1993–95 income statements of Harnischfeger Industries shown in Table 2, the company reported a restructuring charge of $67 million in 1993 and an $8 million item labeled "nonrecurring charge." (Restructuring charges are discussed in the next section of this chapter.) In 1995, the company reported a separate line item for costs associated with a recent merger (together with associated tax costs). An analyst wishing to examine the trend in a company's income from continuing operations must decide how to treat these items.

The easiest alternative (aside from completely ignoring them) is to remove them (with their associated tax effects) from the analysis. In this approach, the analyst is relying on management's classification of the items as one-time or nonrecurring items.

Experience says, however, that a deeper analysis is usually worth conducting. The purpose is to determine what these charges represent, whether they are truly nonrecurring, and whether the charges relate solely to the past or include costs more properly associated with the future. Additionally, analysts will benefit from determining whether the income statement contains "buried" items—items that might properly be considered unusual or nonrecurring but to which management has not explicitly drawn attention.

Where does one obtain the details necessary to carry out such an investigation? The notes to the financial statements and the management discussion and analysis (MD&A) sections of the annual report are good starting points. For example, in the notes to the 1995 financial statements, Harnischfeger explained that the nonrecurring charge in 1993 was for reestimation of certain warranty reserves, as shown in **Exhibit 2**.

   ©2000, The Research Foundation of AIMR

Exhibit 2. Harnischfeger Industries Explanation of 1993 Nonrecurring Charge

The Company recorded a charge in fiscal 1993 resulting from the reestimation of certain warranty reserves carried by the Mining Equipment Division. The charge reduced pre-tax income by $8,000. This nonrecurring charge was the result of a much deeper analysis of open warranty claims and customer requests, field experience on new products, and additional analytical data provided by new systems which has since resulted in engineering, design and manufacturing changes. The Company's warranty methodology, while long established, is by its very nature based on management's judgment and is not mathematically precise or actuarially based. The resultant warranty reserves are reevaluated periodically and reflect refinements of estimated warranty exposure on evolving product lines.

Source: Harnischfeger Industries 1995 annual report.

This explanation suggests that prior years' expenses had been understated (by not accruing a sufficient warranty liability) and, for analytical purposes, ought to be adjusted upward. The information in the note is insufficient to determine the number of periods affected, but if the analyst has knowledge of the company's normal warranty periods, he or she can make a reasonable estimate.

To gain a better understanding of these estimates, an analyst can ask company managers or investor-relations personnel for more detail on the charge. The answers will provide clues to the long-term effects of the warranty issue. For example, is this note evidence of a reduction in the quality of the company's products or of engineering work or evidence of a change in customer perceptions of the company's offerings? These factors are, of course, important for analysts to consider in forecasts of future results.

Another question that arises in reading the 1993 Harnischfeger income data is whether it is merely a coincidence that the company decided to reestimate the warranty reserves in the same year it recorded a restructuring charge. Skeptical analysts will not ignore the charges but, rather, will question whether the company was trying to "take a big bath" in 1993—that is, dump all the bad news into one earnings report in the hope that it will be ignored in future periods. As always, to determine the quality of the company's earnings, analysts need to consider these unexpected adjustments of accounting estimates in light of other accounting practices the company has adopted.

■ *Identifying unusual items.* The notes and MD&A section of the financial statements can help analysts uncover items that are not specifically labeled "unusual" in the statements themselves but that might be considered nonrecurring. For example, the notes to the 1995 Harnischfeger financial statements state that a $29 million gain on the sale of shares in an affiliated company is included in "other income." Management did not flag this gain in the same fashion as it did the losses, but this item seems to be a nonrecurring gain that should be removed from recurring or operating income for analysis purposes. Interestingly, the 1996 Harnischfeger income statement did separately disclose the 1995 gain (and its tax effect) in much the same way it treated the recent merger costs. This step made it easier for readers to assess the persistence of reported earnings—and coincidentally lowered the "expected" level of earnings against which 1996 results might reasonably be compared.

Another example of disclosure of an unusual item makes clear the value of going beyond the income statement alone. In the 1994–96 financial statements of Total Petroleum (North America) Ltd., a number of potentially nonrecurring items are buried in higher-level categories in the income statement and are outlined only in the notes. In 1994 and 1995, the company did not— on the face of the income statement—refer specifically to unusual items that amounted to more than 10 percent of the respective period's net income or loss. Clearly, analysts who ignore the notes do so at their own peril.

As these examples demonstrate, a common unusual item is the restructuring charge, to which we now turn our attention.

Restructurings

> But, some investors and other critics argue that AT&T's fourth major restructuring in the past decade—following big one-time moves in 1986, 1988, and 1991—has left them dazed and confused about how much money the telecommunications giant has actually been making.
>
> — *Smith and Lipin (1996)*

In recent years, restructuring charges have been prominent on the income statements of many companies. [26] For example, recall from Table 2 that

---

[26] An exit cost, or restructuring cost, according to the Financial Accounting Standards Board [Emerging Issues Task Force No. 94-3, "Liability Recognition for Certain Employee Termination Benefits and Other Costs to Exit an Activity (including Certain Costs Incurred in a Restructuring)"], is a cost resulting from a plan to exit an activity that has no future economic benefit. *All* three following conditions need to be met to record a restructuring cost:

1. The cost is not associated with or does not benefit activities that will be continued.

2. The cost is not associated with or is not incurred to generate revenues after the exit plan's commitment date.

3. The cost meets one of the following criteria:

   a. The cost is incremental to other costs incurred by the enterprise in the conduct of its

Harnischfeger reported a restructuring charge of $67 million in fiscal 1993—enough to put operating income into the loss column that year. These charges are typically associated with a decision to "do things differently in the future" and they generally involve layoffs, plant closings, and asset write-downs. The difficulty in dealing with restructuring charges is not trying to discover them; normally, they are clearly labeled on the income statement. The trick is to get a handle on what they represent and what they suggest about the future. Indeed, the Emerging Issues Task Force (EITF) of the Financial Accounting Standards Board (FASB) deliberated on this matter because the members believed that many companies were including inappropriate items in their restructuring charges. As a result, since 1994, stricter guidance exists for what can and cannot be included in restructuring charges, when they are accrued, and how they are disclosed.[27]

Determining *when* to accrue for restructuring and *what* to include in the charge is difficult and fraught with uncertainty. Managers who believe that investors and analysts discount the impact of restructuring charges have an incentive to increase the charge ("it's already $1 billion, why not make it $1.2 billion?"). That way, in future years, costs can be charged against the restructuring liability instead of earnings. If the restructuring charge has been overaccrued in one year, it can be brought back into income in a future year, perhaps with the intent to raise or smooth those earnings.

---

activities prior to the commitment date and will be incurred as a direct result of the exit plan (e.g., the additional cost of subcontracting warranty work over the cost that would be incurred had the company continued to provide the service itself *or* the costs of employees and other costs to be incurred to close a plant after it ceases operations).

b. The cost represents amounts to be incurred by the enterprise under a contractual obligation that existed prior to the commitment date and will either continue after the exit plan is completed with no economic benefit to the enterprise or be a penalty to cancel the contractual obligation (e.g., a lease cancellation penalty or the cost of leased space that will remain unused for the duration of a lease once the exit plan is completed).

[27]The guidance is included in EITF No. 94-3 (see previous footnote in this chapter). Other guidance is provided in, among others, EITF No. 96-9, "Classification of Inventory Markdowns and Other Costs Associated with a Restructuring"; No. 95-23, "The Treatment of Certain Site Restoration/Environmental Exit Costs When Testing a Long-Lived Asset for Impairment"; and No. 95-3, "Recognition of Liabilities in Connection with a Purchase Business Combination." In the U.S. Securities and Exchange Commission's Staff Accounting Bulletin (SAB) No. 100, the SEC reiterated that restructuring charges need to be charged only when rigorously developed and thoroughly supported plans to exit an activity exist. In SAB No. 100, the SEC is cracking down on the practice of accruing large charges in poor periods with the hope that such expenses will be ignored in future analyses. Formal documentation and approval by upper-level managers of the specifics of the restructuring are required before an accrual can be recorded. Furthermore, enhanced disclosure in the footnotes and MD&A of the status of the accruals (and their reversals) needs to be presented in future interim and annual financial statements.

EITF No. 94-3 (together with the guidance of the U.S. Securities and Exchange Commission's Staff Accounting Bulletin [SAB] No. 100) attempts to add a degree of uniformity to the types of costs included in restructuring charges—in particular, to stop companies from including the restructuring charge costs that more properly relate to future years.[28] For example, the cost of layoffs can be accrued as a liability and charged as part of the restructuring expense only when *all* the following conditions exist:

- Prior to the date of the financial statements, management, having the appropriate level of authority to impose involuntary termination on employees, approves and commits the enterprise to the plan of termination and establishes the benefits that current employees will receive upon termination.
- Prior to the date of the financial statements, the benefit arrangement is communicated in detail to employees.
- The plan of termination specifically identifies the number of employees to be terminated, their job classifications or functions, and their locations.
- The period of time to complete the plan of termination indicates that significant changes to the plan of termination are not likely.

Similar criteria need to be met to accrue other sorts of restructuring charges.

Contrary to most accounting standards, which promote conservatism that results in income understatement, this guidance effectively delays the recognition of expenses. The main reason for this position in the standards is that some companies had been accruing a variety of *future* costs (such as marketing campaigns for the company's "new image," updated information systems installed to enhance productivity in the restructured company, and so on) with their restructuring charges in the hope that the entire charge would be discounted by analysts as a one-time event. The resulting *early* recognition of expenses would lead to future earnings being higher than otherwise.

From an accounting perspective, restructurings are neither extraordinary items nor discontinued operations. As we will see, those items are reported on a net-of-tax basis, and per-share data for the items are also reported. Standard setters expressed concern that companies would try to blur the distinction between restructuring and these other items. Because, in principle, restructurings are conceptually distinct from discontinued

---

[28]Despite the EITF's attempt to tighten the rules, skeptical analysts and the business press often uncover suspicious items related to restructurings. For example, Laing (1998) questioned components of Sunbeam's 1996 restructuring charge. He noted large increases in litigation reserves and the allowance for doubtful accounts. This *Barron's* article is widely credited with the firing of CEO Al Dunlap and the initiation of a Securities and Exchange Commission inquiry into the company's accounting methods.

     ©2000, The Research Foundation of AIMR

operations (i.e., restructurings represent a new way of engaging in a continuing line of business, and a discontinued operation is a line of business that will no longer be engaged in) and are not unusual and infrequent (the accountant's definition of extraordinary), their disclosure ought not lead to confusion among the categories. As such, standard setters concluded that for restructuring costs, the following conditions should apply:

- The income statement effect of recognizing a liability at the commitment date should be reported in income from continuing operations and should *not* be reported on the face of the income statement net of income taxes.
- The effect on earnings per share should *not* be disclosed on the face of the income statement.
- Revenue and related costs and expenses of activities that will not be continued should *not* be combined and reported as a separate component of income.

In addition, the following information, when material, must be disclosed:

- A description of the major actions composing the exit plan, activities that will not be continued, including the method of disposition and the anticipated date of completion.
- A description of the type and amount of exit costs recognized as liabilities and the classification of those costs in the income statement.
- A description of the type and amount of exit costs paid and charged against the liability.
- The amount of any adjustment(s) to the liability.
- For all periods presented, the revenue and net operating income or losses from activities that will not be continued, if those activities have separately identifiable operations.

The key to dealing with restructuring charges is to understand what they are for, why they are needed, and what will be different in the future. Reaching such understanding can be a nontrivial and time-consuming task. In assessing possible future changes, analysts need to ask whether they have seen the last of the charges or whether the company is one of many that recognizes "*recurring* nonrecurring charges." This judgment should be a function of prior experience with the company and the disclosures made by the company. Analysts should administer a healthy dose of skepticism to disclosures and descriptions provided by companies that have a history of recurring nonrecurring items.

A two-step approach to the analysis of restructuring costs is useful. The first step is to determine which charges relate to the past and which to the future so that appropriate adjustments to historical trends can be made. In reading the financial press, company press releases, and analysts' research reports, one sometimes gets the feeling that the best thing to do with restructuring charges is to ignore them. Analysts should resist this temptation because these charges often reflect the cumulative effect of items that should have been charged off in the past. For example, when the charges represent the cost of closing a factory or disposing of equipment, it suggests that prior-period depreciation expense was too low and that the level of prior earnings thus was too high. A simple way to deal with the charge is to allocate it to, say, the past five years and restate prior results for analysis purposes. Although somewhat arbitrary, this method seems better than ignoring the costs altogether. Lowenstein (1997) suggests that analysts should add up the restructuring charges of the past five years, average them, penalize each prior quarter by the same amount, and in the future, deduct the same charge from expected earnings. His logic is that businesses almost always make mistakes, and although such errors do not happen every 90 days, they are nonetheless to be expected. The second step in the analysis of restructuring charges is to monitor the reserves and their uses from prior years to assess the veracity of prior disclosures, the likelihood that prior restructurings are on track, and whether the planned savings are materializing.

A critical item to look for is the reversal of old restructuring charges into current-period earnings. Companies that have carefully called attention to their so-called nonrecurring restructurings in prior periods have been known to be less forthcoming when the charges are reversed in later years.[29] Prudent analysts will be on the lookout for reversals buried in cost of sales or selling and administrative expenses.

In some ways, restructuring charges are similar in spirit to discontinuing certain operations of the company. From an accounting perspective, the major difference between restructuring and discontinuing operations is one of intent and scope. Restructurings rearrange the way business is done and sometimes that means incurring exit costs related to facility closures and downsizing. Nonetheless, the company does not exit the businesses it is engaged in. Discontinued operations involve leaving entire lines of business, and we turn to this topic in the next section.

---

[29] These reversals take place whenever the estimated cost of the restructuring turns out to be too large. The exit plan is completed, but a portion of the initial accrued liability remains. Reversing the liability leads to "negative" expenses being recorded. Most analysts would not consider them recurring benefits.

        ©2000, The Research Foundation of AIMR

Discontinued Operations

> MacMillan Bloedel said it agreed to sell its paper-making unit for $850 million Canadian dollars to a group of investors. . . . MacMillan said the sale will result in a charge of C$35 to C$45 million, to be recorded in discontinued operations in the second quarter.
>
> —*Chipello (1998)*

Analysts should be on the lookout for restructurings that are classified as discontinued operations. Restructurings are admissions on the part of management that the way business was done in the past needs to change in order to be effective in the future. Often, such a change means that prior-period results were misstated. (For example, assets may have been depreciated over estimated useful lives that turned out to have been too long.) Consequently, restructurings include costs that might otherwise be considered recurring but are simply aggregated into a single year. In addition, because they typically involve significant accounting estimates, any changes in the estimates are dealt with prospectively and prior-period results are not restated. Diligent analysts, however, will carefully consider the effects of any changes in estimates.

Discontinued operations are different from restructurings and involve changes in operations for which the past truly may not be representative of the future. Accountants restate prior results and accord special treatment to gains and losses on disposal of these operations. Management, in turn, has incentives to treat charges that might be classified as restructuring costs as costs of discontinued operations to obtain this accounting treatment. Thus, the careful analyst will be on the lookout for the gray areas and will carefully examine the nature of the charges involved in discontinued operations disclosures. Accounting guidance for these activities is found in APB (Accounting Principles Board) Opinion 30, *Reporting the Results of Operations—Reporting the Effects of Disposal of a Segment of a Business, and Extraordinary, Unusual and Infrequently Occurring Events and Transactions.*

Companies add and drop product lines as part of the normal course of business. Revenues and expenses related to the disposal of *part* of a business, the shifting of production or marketing activities from one line or location to another, the phasing out of a product or service, and changes driven by technological improvements are not considered discontinued operations. These are considered normal costs of continuing operations. For companies in today's business environment, avoiding such costs while remaining competitive is difficult to imagine. In contrast, companies may decide to fundamentally change the mix of economic activity for their overall organization and dispose of an entire business segment.

Special accounting is required if a disposal qualifies as a business segment. APB Opinion 30 defines a "segment of a business" as a component of an entity whose activities represent a separate major line of business or class of customer. Opinion 30 provides the following examples of disposals that should be classified as disposals of a segment of a business:

- A diversified company sells a major division that represents the company's only activities in the electronics industry.
- A meatpacking company sells a 25 percent interest in a professional football team that has been accounted for under the equity method. All other activities of the company are in the meatpacking business.
- A communications company sells all its radio stations. The company's remaining activities are three television stations and a publishing company. The assets and results of operations of the radio stations are clearly distinguishable physically, operationally, and for financial reporting purposes.
- A food distributor disposes of one of its two divisions. One division sells food wholesale, primarily to supermarket chains, and the other division sells food through its chain of fast-food restaurants, some of which are franchised and some of which are company owned. Both divisions are in the business of food distribution, but the nature of selling food through fast-food outlets is vastly different from that of wholesaling food to supermarket chains. By having two major classes of customers, the company has two segments of its business.

Furthermore, the following disposals are *not* classified as disposals of a segment of a business.

- A mining company sells a foreign subsidiary engaged in silver mining that represents all of the controlling company's activities in a particular country. The fact that the company continues to engage in silver mining activities in other countries indicates that the sale represents only a part of a line of business.
- A petrochemical company sells a 25 percent interest in a petrochemical plant. Because the remaining activities of the company are in the same line of business as the 25 percent interest that has been sold, the transaction is a sale not of a major line of business but of only part of a line of business.
- A diversified company sells a subsidiary that manufactures furniture. The company has retained its other furniture-manufacturing subsidiary. The disposal of the subsidiary, therefore, is not a disposal of a segment of the business but rather a disposal of part of a line of business. Such disposals are incidental to the evolution of the entity's business.

©2000, The Research Foundation of AIMR

- The sale of all the assets related to the manufacture of men's woolen suits by an apparel manufacturer in order to concentrate activities in the manufacture of men's suits from synthetic products. This transaction would represent a disposal of a product line, as distinguished from the disposal of a major line of business.

Disclosures about discontinued operations involve two relevant dates. The measurement date is the date at which the decision to discontinue an operation is made. The disposal date is the date at which the operation is sold or abandoned. Sometimes these dates coincide, but more often, they do not. The period between the two is known as the phase-out period. In the reporting period that includes the measurement date, the results of discontinued operations prior to the measurement date are disclosed separately from continuing operations and net of tax. Prior-period data are restated as well. This approach allows the analyst to see more clearly the trend in continuing operations.

In addition, a gain or loss on the disposal is recorded in the same period as the measurement date. The calculation of the gain or loss depends on whether the disposal and measurement dates coincide, whether the disposal and measurement dates are in the same period, and whether a net gain or loss is expected. When the measurement and disposal dates coincide, the gain or loss is separately disclosed, net of tax. When the measurement and disposal dates are different but occur in the same period, results of the discontinued operations between the measurement date and the disposal date are netted with the gain or loss on the sale of the net assets to arrive at the net gain or loss on disposal (reported net of tax). Details of each component are provided.

When the two dates fall in different periods, management needs to estimate the results of operations up to the (possibly unknown) disposal date and the gain or loss on the net asset sale. When the (expected) combined results of the discontinued operations subsequent to the measurement date and the gain or loss on the disposal of the net assets sum to a net loss, the entire amount is accrued in the same period as the measurement date. Thus, as long as the *sum* of the expected operating profits or losses and expected gain or loss on net asset sale is a net loss, the net amount is conservatively reported, even though the amounts may occur in later periods. When net gains are expected, the gains are recorded only when realized.

From the perspective of an equity analyst valuing a company, the discontinued operations disclosures offer an opportunity to break earnings into persistent and transitory components. In most cases, the disposals take place over a relatively short period. When the discontinued operations spill over into future periods and the amounts are material, analysts should separately value the continuing and discontinued operations. The accounting disclosures of net assets of discontinued operations and separate disclosure of operating results are particularly amenable to analysis by using the DAE model.

As if the confusion in determining what is unusual and what is discontinued were not enough, accountants have another category of items that appears on the income statement: extraordinary items. According to APB Opinion 30, an event or transaction should be classified as extraordinary if it is both *unusual* and *infrequent*.[30] "Unusual" implies that the event or transaction is highly abnormal and not related to, or incidentally related to, the ordinary activities of the enterprise. "Infrequent" implies that the event or transaction is not expected to recur in the foreseeable future.

Extraordinary Items. Assessing whether an item is unusual and infrequent requires consideration of the context in which it arose. For example, one might consider the Exxon Valdez oil spill to be unusual and infrequent on the basis of its magnitude. Further thought, however, leads one to realize that major oil companies likely spill *some* oil daily. Indeed, oil companies undoubtedly devote part of their risk-management activities to ensuring an effective cost–benefit trade-off for spills. In this light, it is not surprising that Exxon Corporation did *not* report the related costs of the spill as extraordinary. Rather, as shown in **Table 3**, the company reported the item on a separate line of the income statement (i.e., as an unusual item).

APB Opinion 30 indicates that certain items are *not* considered extraordinary, including

- write-down or write-off of receivables, inventories, equipment leased to others, deferred research and development costs, and other intangible assets;
- gains and losses from exchange or translation of foreign currencies, including those related to major devaluations or revaluations;
- gains and losses on the disposal of a segment of a business;

---

[30]This definition is subtly different from the one used in International Accounting Standard No. 8, which defines extraordinary items as "income or expenses that arise from events or transactions that are clearly distinct from the ordinary activities of the enterprise and, therefore, are not expected to recur frequently or regularly." The difference in definitions underscores our contention that the labeling of income statement items is largely irrelevant, except for contracting purposes. What is important is that the analyst consider the underlying economics of the events in question and comes to a reasoned conclusion about their effect on the profitability of the enterprise.

                    ©2000, The Research Foundation of AIMR

Table 3. Exxon Corporation Consolidated Statements of Income
(millions of dollars)

	1988	1989	1990
Revenue			
Sales and other operating revenue, including excise taxes	$87,252	$95,173	$115,794
Earnings from equity interests and other revenue	1,311	1,112	1,146
Total revenue	$88,563	$96,285	$116,940
Costs and other deductions			
Crude oil and product purchases	33,558	39,268	50,746
Operating expenses	9,968	10,535	11,995
Selling, general, and administrative expenses	5,824	6,398	7,776
Depreciation and depletion	4,790	5,002	5,545
Exploration expenses, including dry holes	979	872	957
Interest expense	944	1,265	1,300
Valdez provision	—	2,545	—
Income taxes	3,124	2,028	3,170
Excise taxes	7,695	8,517	10,275
Other taxes and duties	16,151	16,617	19,894
Income applicable to minority and preferred interests	270	263	272
Total deductions	$83,303	$93,310	$111,930
Income before cumulative effect of accounting change	5,260	2,975	5,010
Cumulative effect of change in accounting for income taxes	—	535	—
Net Income	$ 5,260	$ 3,510	$ 5,010

Note: For years ended December 31.

Source: Exxon Corporation 1990 annual report.

- other gains and losses from sale of abandonment of property, plant, or equipment used in the business;
- effects of a strike, including those against competitors and major suppliers;
- adjustment of accruals on long-term contracts.

In general, most events and transactions will not meet the definition of extraordinary.[31]

When extraordinary items are reported, they are shown as net of income taxes in a separate section of the income statement. In addition, the per-share effect of the items is reported. Note that disclosure is normally provided to enhance the reader's understanding of the event or transaction. For example, refer again to the Harnischfeger income statement reproduced in Table 2 and the excerpt from the related note to the financial statements in **Exhibit 3**. In both fiscal 1994 and 1995, the company retired some of its debt early, but because the cost of doing so exceeded the book value of the debt, a loss was incurred. Analysts reviewing the financial statements and coming across an extraordinary loss should ask why the company has chosen to refinance, how the refinancing was accomplished, and how future results may be affected. For example, has the company been able to restructure the debt with cheaper debt or with less restrictive debt? Is the company timing the retirement to achieve some sort of income smoothing? Was the debt refinanced because of (or to avoid) the violation of a covenant?[32]

Accounting Changes

Generally accepted accounting principles (GAAP) allow considerable flexibility in their application. Although the maintained assumption is that companies follow the same rules on a consistent basis, companies may adopt different rules from one year to the next. These changes can be classified in two categories—mandatory and voluntary.

Mandatory Accounting Changes. Mandatory accounting changes arise because of the issuance of a new accounting standard. Sometimes new standards require retroactive adjustment (i.e., a restatement of prior financial statements as though the new rules had been in place in prior periods) and sometimes prospective adjustment is needed (i.e., from the period of issuance forward, the new rule is in effect). When prospective application of a new standard is put in place (for example, recent standards dealing with income

---

[31]Some items are explicitly defined as extraordinary. Interestingly, (as we will see in our Harnischfeger example) the gain or loss that arises on the early retirement of debt is, by definition, treated as an extraordinary item (in accordance with SFAS No. 4, *Reporting Gains and Losses from Extinguishment of Debt*).

[32]Research by Hand (1989) suggests that companies used debt–equity swaps to smooth an unexpected and transitory decrease in earnings per share. These findings may generalize to other debt-related activity. Skeptical analysts will consider management's motives for early debt retirement in order to assess whether the transactions were undertaken for economic or accounting purposes.

 ©2000, The Research Foundation of AIMR

Exhibit 3. Harnischfeger Industries Extraordinary Item Disclosure

Note 7: Long-Term Obligations, Bank Credit Facilities, and Interest Expense (excerpts)

On December 29, 1994, Joy issued an offer to purchase for cash at 101 percent any and all of its outstanding 10 1/4 percent senior notes. This offer expired on February 10, 1995, with $270 being redeemed under the offer. Prior to this tender offer, the company had purchased $11,350 of outstanding 10 1/4 percent senior notes in unsolicited open market transactions. As a result of the bank facility and 10 1/4 percent senior note redemptions (see below), the company recorded an extraordinary loss on debt retirement, net of applicable income taxes, of $3,481 or $0.08 per share, consisting primarily of unamortized financing costs and redemption premiums.

During fiscal 1994, the company recorded an extraordinary after-tax charge of $4,827 associated with the prepayment of Joy's outstanding Tranche A term loans existing under the bank facility and all of Joy's 12.3 percent junior subordinated notes. This charge is comprised of the write-off of the unamortized discount and unamortized capitalized financing costs, call premiums, and other expenses. The remaining borrowings outstanding under the bank facility were repaid in full on November 29, 1994, upon the consummation of the company's merger with Joy. The Tranche A term loans carried an interest rate of 2.125 percent above LIBOR[a], and the Tranche B term loan had a floating interest rate equal, at Joy's option, to the base rate plus 2 percent or to the eurodollar rate plus 3 percent. The bank facility agreement, including its revolving credit agreement, was terminated concurrent with the merger.

[a]LIBOR (London Interbank Offered Rate).

Source: Harnischfeger Industries 1995 annual report.

---

taxes and postretirement benefits), a one-time adjustment is made for prior years to "catch up."

For example, consider GTE Corporation's 1992 Income Statement, which includes a charge to current-period income of $2.4 billion. This amount relates to the company's application of SFAS No. 106, *Employers' Accounting for Postretirement Benefits Other Than Pensions*, commonly known as OPEB (other postemployment benefits). This standard requires companies to change from pay-as-you-go (effectively, cash-basis) accounting for health care benefits to the accrual method. This change meant that postretirement benefits promised and earned by employees in prior years that had never been recorded as expenses or liabilities needed to be accrued. SFAS No. 106 requires companies to make a single cumulative adjustment for prior-year expenses, rather than estimate the cost and year-end liability in each of the prior years and restate the prior financial statements (i.e., retroactive restatements of the balance sheet and income statement were not required). Thus, GTE's current-period income statement reports OPEB costs in two places. First, among the operating expenses for 1992, OPEB costs are measured on an accrual basis. This measurement makes comparisons with 1991 and prior years difficult because the OPEB costs were recorded on a cash basis in those years. Second, the cumulative adjustment reported in 1992 income captures all prior unrecorded expenses and charges them against current-period profits.

Often, companies and the analysts who follow them indicate that those cumulative adjustments should be ignored. After all, they say, the charges are "one-time" and "noncash." Although simply ignoring the cumulative adjustment may make sense in analyzing current-year performance, it does not consider that prior-year costs have been understated. As such, when evaluations of year-over-year trends are made, as well as measures of absolute performance levels, analysts *need* to consider how the financial statements would have looked if retroactive adjustment had been made. Companies rarely provide precise figures to allow such adjustments. Nonetheless, one can start by applying the current-year effect, if provided, to the prior years' financial statements (perhaps with an adjustment for inflation or, in the case of OPEB, workforce levels). This strategy is similar to the one we suggested for dealing with restructuring costs and other so-called one-time events that, in fact, suggest that prior-period results may have been overstated (see Lowenstein 1997).[33]

Voluntary Accounting Changes and Changes in Accounting Estimates. Voluntary accounting changes need to be treated with caution. Analysts need to determine why a company is changing its accounting policies. Reasonable explanations include changing to use policies generally used by competitors and rationalizing different policies that might arise as acquisitions take place. Although these reasons may be valid, analysts should always question the timing of the changes and evaluate them in light of any other issues related to quality of earnings. For example, in fiscal 1996, B/E Aerospace changed its method of accounting for engineering costs. Rather than capitalize and amortize the costs, the company began to expense them immediately, consistent with its competitors. The skeptical analyst will question the timing of such a change. In this case, the company was otherwise having a very poor year. Was it dumping all its bad news into one announcement? Did the new method enhance the usefulness of the firm's reporting?

Voluntary accounting changes normally involve restating prior results, although some companies argue that the differences are not material. Voluntary changes in accounting method can be distinguished from changes in accounting estimates. Changing the inventory-cost allocation method from FIFO (first in, first out) to LIFO (last in, first out) or the depreciation method

---

[33]Furthermore, to the extent that the new accounting standard provides management with new information, they may make different operating decisions. It is widely believed that the adoption of new OPEB measurement requirements led many companies to change the way they managed their OPEB costs.

from accelerated to straight line is a change in method. Changing the estimate of obsolete inventory or the estimated useful life of equipment is a change in estimate. Changes in estimate are accounted for prospectively (that is, prior results are not restated). Sometimes, pro forma figures are provided. As with voluntary accounting changes, the important thing for the analyst to consider is the reason for the change in estimates and whether the change is intended to improve the quality of the disclosures or to mislead analysts. The change in estimates could be timed to record a "big bath," thereby alleviating the need for the company to amortize the costs in future years.

Comprehensive Income and Its Components

For fiscal years beginning after December 15, 1997, companies are required to report a reconciliation of net income to comprehensive income in the primary financial statements. In SFAS No. 130, comprehensive income is defined as:

> the change in equity [net assets] of a business enterprise during a period from transactions and other events and circumstances from nonowner sources. It includes all changes in equity during a period, except those resulting from investments by owners and distributions to owners.[34]

If all such nonowner transactions ran through the income statement, comprehensive income would be identical to net income.

The required explicit reconciliation of comprehensive income to net income is partly in response to concerns that an increasing number of earnings-related items were being reported in varying locations throughout the financial statements. The SFAS No. 130 reporting requirements are designed to reduce the effort required to find and analyze these other performance-related items. The FASB did not specify the format and financial statement location of the comprehensive income reconciliation, so companies can include the information as an extension of the income statement, a stand-alone statement of performance, or as part of the statement of changes in equity. Most companies have elected to report it as part of the statement of changes in equity.

The most common cause of direct changes to equity is recording assets and liabilities at market value (or some modified market value) on the balance sheet. For example, when available-for-sale marketable securities are recorded at market value, unrealized gains and losses are included on the balance sheet as part of "accumulated other comprehensive income" and in the reconciliation of net and comprehensive income as "other comprehensive income." When the securities are sold, the realized gain or loss is recorded on the income statement. To avoid double counting the gain in both this

---

[34] Brackets are in the original text.

period's net income and a prior period's comprehensive income, "other comprehensive income" includes a reclassification adjustment in the period of the realized gain.

Other items included in other comprehensive income are adjustments for foreign currency exchange rate changes, minimum pension liability adjustments, and derivatives-related hedging activities. Most of the items included in the reconciliation are outside of management's control (i.e., the company may manage foreign currency risk, but it is unlikely to be able to affect the exchange rates themselves). One exception is the net unrealized gain on available-for-sale marketable securities. That is, although a company may not be able to influence security prices, it can strategically time the sale of securities with previously unrealized gains or losses (a practice known as "cherry picking"). The strategically-timed sales will not affect comprehensive income, because a reclassification adjustment is made so that the gains are not counted in comprehensive income twice (once as other comprehensive income and once as net income). For example, **Table 4** shows the 1997 adjustments First Indiana Corporation made in its report of comprehensive income.[35]

Nonetheless, current-period net income can be managed via the strategic timing of sales of available-for-sale marketable securities.[36] Consequently, the clear reporting of marketable securities activity (one of the components of other comprehensive income) can help analysts assess the quality of a company's reported net income.

---

[35]In 1997, First Indiana's net income was $17,744 and its comprehensive income was $18,797 (figures in thousands). The difference is attributable to two items. First, the company received a tax benefit when certain stock options were exercised. These transactions did not affect earnings, but the tax benefit positively affected shareholders. Second, the company recorded a net unrealized holding gain on its available-for-sale marketable securities portfolio of $614 (net of tax). This unrealized gain appears in equity but bypasses the income statement. When the securities are sold, the realized gain will appear in net income and thus flow through to retained earnings. To avoid double-counting the gains (i.e., once as unrealized gains and once as realized ones), when the securities are sold, previously recorded unrealized gains that were included in equity as accumulated other comprehensive income are reversed. At First Indiana, the 1997 reversals out of accumulated other comprehensive income (and included in net income) were $217 (net of tax).

[36]Of course, we are not implying that all sales of marketable securities are strategic and are made to manage earnings. Clearly, however, some analysts do look for such activity. Referring to a series of one-time gains that allowed Citicorp to report a 12 percent increase in 1997 fourth-quarter earnings as "hamburger helper," an analyst quoted in the *Wall Street Journal's* "Heard on the Street" column singled out securities gains as one reason why Citicorp's earnings for the period were considered of poor quality (see Frank and Browning 1998). More recently, Microsoft Corporation's earnings quality has come under scrutiny as the level of marketable security activity has increased (see Bank 2000).

                                                       ©2000, The Research Foundation of AIMR

Summary

Determining the quality and persistence of earnings is tricky. It requires not only in-depth knowledge of a company's competitive strategy and its relationship to its industry and competitors but also knowledge of the accounting rules used to generate earnings reports. Prudent analysts are aware that management has both the incentive and the discretion to practice opportunistic earnings management in both the classification and the timing of certain elements of earnings. Analysis of the notes to the financial statements, a careful reading of management's discussion and analysis, and a healthy dose of skepticism go a long way toward generating an understanding of past earnings trends and the questions for management to aid in the development of forecasted future results.

We believe that accounting classifications are especially useful starting points for understanding the nature or persistence of earnings. Nonetheless, it is important for analysts to look beyond the classifications to get at the underlying events. In this chapter, we outlined the categories of income typically found in U.S. GAAP earnings reports. We described the classification rules and provided guidance to analysts with respect to interpreting the data and restating them for fundamental analysis purposes. The key to analysis of recurring and nonrecurring items is the determination of their effect on future earnings and cash flows, and thus, the value of the company.

Table 4. First Indiana Corporation's Comprehensive Income Disclosures, 1997
(dollars in thousands, except per-share data)

Item	Common Stock		Paid-In Capital in Excess of Par	Retained Earnings	Accumulated Other Comprehensive Income	Treasury Stock	Total Shareholders' Equity
	Shares	Amount					
Balance at December 31, 1994	12,974,854	$131	$31,867	$88,981	($120)	($147)	$120,712
1995 comprehensive income							
Net earnings for 1995	—	—	—	17,267	—	—	17,267
Unrealized gain on securities available for sale, net of income taxes of $351 and reclassification adjustment (Note 2)	—	—	—	—	515	—	515
Total comprehensive income							$17,782
Common stock issued under restricted stock plans, net of amortization (Note 13)	—	—	268	99	—	—	367
Common stock issued under deferred compensation plan	—	—	—	(21)	—	—	(21)
Exercise of stock options	120,830	1	536	—	—	—	537
Dividends—$0.32 per share	—	—	—	(3,877)	—	—	(3,877)
Purchase of treasury stock	(687,199)	—	—	—	—	(6,203)	(6,203)
Balance at December 31, 1995	12,408,485	$132	$32,671	$102,449	$395	($6,350)	$129,297
1996 comprehensive income							
Net earnings for 1996	—	—	—	13,704	—	—	13,704
Unrealized loss on securities available for sale, net of income taxes of ($320) and reclassification adjustment (Note 2)	—	—	—	—	(467)	—	(467)
Total comprehensive income							$13,237
Common stock issued under restricted stock plans, net of amortization (Note 13)	—	—	195	278	—	—	473
Common stock issued under deferred compensation plan	—	—	—	(20)	—	—	(20)
Exercise of stock options	47,701	—	331	—	—	—	331
Dividends—$0.38 per share	—	—	—	(4,644)	—	—	(4,644)
Payment for fractional shares	(1,064)	—	(16)	—	—	—	(16)
Balance at December 31, 1996	12,455,122	$132	$33,181	$111,767	($72)	($6,350)	$138,658

©2000, The Research Foundation of AIMR

Table 4. (continued)

Item	Common Stock		Paid-In Capital in Excess of Par	Retained Earnings	Accumulated Other Comprehensive Income	Treasury Stock	Total Shareholders' Equity
	Shares	Amount					
1997 comprehensive income							
Net earnings for 1997	—	—	—	17,744	—	—	17,744
Unrealized gain on securities available for sale, net of income taxes of $271 and reclassification adjustment (Note 2)	—	—	—	—	397	—	397
Tax benefit of stock options exercised	—	—	—	—	656	—	656
Total comprehensive income							$18,797
Common stock issued under restricted stock plans, net of amortization (Note 13)	43,500	—	1,088	(725)	—	—	363
Common stock issued under deferred compensation plan	—	—	—	(24)	—	—	(24)
Exercise of stock options	201,306	2	866	—	—	—	868
Dividends—$0.40 per share	—	—	—	(5,063)	—	—	(5,063)
Redemption of common stock	(29,823)	—	(501)	—	—	—	(501)
Purchase of treasury stock	(6,000)	—	—	—	—	(132)	(132)
Reissuance of treasury stock	4,591	—	40	—	—	42	82
Payment for fractional shares	(505)	—	(12)	—	—	—	(12)
Balance at December 31, 1997	12,668,191	$134	$34,662	$123,699	$981	($6,440)	$153,036

The following table was included in Note 2 to the financial statements:

	December 31		
	1997	1996	1995
Unrealized holding gains (losses) arising during the period	$614	($186)	$568
Reclassification adjustment for gains included in net earnings	(217)	(281)	(53)
Net unrealized gain (loss) on securities available for sale	$397	($467)	$515

Note: Consolidated statements of shareholders' equity.

Source: First Indiana Corporation and subsidiaries 1997 annual report.

Chapter 3. How Buy-Side Equity Analysts Use Earnings in Valuation

In this chapter, we report the results of an experiment in which we provided buy-side equity analysts with financial information and asked them to value the common stock of a hypothetical company. Most valuation-related research in finance and accounting is based on the analysis of complex mathematical models (i.e., analytical research) or involves the study of historical databases, such as stock prices and published accounting information (i.e., archival research). Although less frequently conducted, controlled experiments (i.e., experimental research) can provide powerful and complementary evidence about cause-and-effect relationships in valuation. In the experiment described in this chapter, we provided different subgroups of analysts with subtly different income information for the hypothetical company and kept constant all other financial information (e.g., balance sheet and cash flows). This approach not only allows inferences about the general role of earnings in valuation but also makes it possible to isolate the incremental importance of reported income and its components in equity analysts' valuation activities.[37]

Although experiments cannot capture all elements of the naturally occurring settings to which one wants to generalize, the method allows precise manipulation of the variables of interest and control of variables that are not of interest. This ability provides an important advantage over methods that rely on analysis of archival databases. For example, in the experiment we report, we designed a set of case materials in which the company to be valued was the same in all versions, except that we seeded a type of earnings management into a subset of the versions. This approach allowed us to investigate the use of accounting earnings and its components while significantly reducing the

---

[37]We did not analyze sell-side analysts' reports because, in addition to valuing and recommending stocks, they usually make explicit forecasts for future-period earnings. Thus, even if sell-side analysts completely ignore earnings in their valuation activities (e.g., by using a pure dividend discount model or free cash flow approach), one would expect many references to a company's past earnings performance in support of the report's forecast of future-period earnings.

possibility that "real" economic differences in the companies caused differences in analysts' stock-price judgments. Experiments also allow investigation of economic phenomena when archival data are sparse or not yet available. In this study, we are able to investigate the role of various types of financial information in the valuation judgments of buy-side analysts, despite the fact that the valuation activities of these analysts typically are not publicly disclosed.

Finally, although archival research can show the "real world" effect of information on investor decisions through stock returns (i.e., executed buy and sell decisions determine price), traditional research methods cannot as readily provide evidence on the judgment process that precedes those decisions. In our experiment, we are able to examine the effect of earnings and other financial information on the stock-price judgments of practicing analysts. For buy-side analysts, the trade data generated after institutional buy or sell orders have been executed constitute the only evidence about these judgments that is available to archival researchers.

Analysts are important consumers of accounting information. Understanding *what* earnings-related information analysts use and *how* that information is actually incorporated into their valuation activities can help analysts recognize and avoid common pitfalls in the interpretation and use of financial accounting information. In addition, a clearer understanding of how analysts use information in their valuation activities can help the Financial Accounting Standards Board (FASB) and the U.S. Securities and Exchange Commission (SEC) in evaluating new and existing financial reporting rules.

Objectives and Procedures

For most fundamental analysts, a logical starting point for predicting the future earnings of a company is the most recent historical earnings of the company. To estimate future earnings, an analyst must assess the various components of the company's historical earnings and decide whether these components will recur and, if so, for how long. Excessive attention to a company's bottom line—without evaluating the individual items that contribute to net income—could lead to an overly optimistic or pessimistic estimate of the future earnings potential of a company. One of the objectives of our experiment, therefore, is to investigate the extent to which analysts recognize the varying persistence of earnings components and take into account significant nonrecurring income items.

An important assumption underlying this chapter is that buy-side analysts actually use reported earnings to value a company. Although the majority of equity analysts likely do not rely *solely* on earnings-based valuation approaches, the innumerable references to earnings and price-to-earnings

©2000, The Research Foundation of AIMR

ratios (P/Es) in sell-side analyst reports and in the financial press suggest that reported income is a nontrivial input of the valuation process. Because little direct evidence exists about the use and relative importance of reported earnings in the activities of individual analysts, another objective of the experiment is to assess the relative importance of earnings information and other potentially useful types of financial statement information.

Financial statement analysis can be a difficult and onerous task. Beyond the inherent uncertainty involved in trying to map financial fundamentals into equity security value, the process is made more difficult by the possibility that a company's reported financial information is not representative of its "true" current economic state or future economic potential. Consistent with this possibility, numerous articles in the financial press and academic research journals indicate that companies manage their earnings in an attempt to influence investors' impressions of the company.[38] If analysts do not detect *opportunistic* earnings management in a company's reporting of past earnings, their predictions of the company's future earnings may be overly optimistic or pessimistic. If historical earnings, or biased estimates of future earnings, are used in valuation models, analysts' assessments of value also may be overly optimistic or pessimistic.

To investigate buy-side analysts' use of earnings information in valuation, we designed an experiment in which we systematically varied certain earnings data and asked analysts to value a security. In particular, we varied the level of opportunistic earnings management in the case materials to determine the potential effect of such a reporting strategy on analysts' valuation judgments. Although many methods of earnings management exist, our investigation is limited to the effect of realized marketable securities gains on analysts' valuation judgments.

Most industrial companies in the United States hold the majority of their marketable equity securities in an "available-for-sale" portfolio. Under current accounting practice, available-for-sale marketable equity securities are included on the balance sheet at fair value. A problem inherent in any type of fair value asset accounting is the treatment of holding gains or losses caused by changes in the assets' fair values.[39] Under Statement of Financial

---

[38] In an article on General Electric Company's earnings management practices, Smith, Lipin, and Naj (1994) provide the following definition of earnings management: "The orchestrated timing of gains and losses to smooth out bumps and, especially, avoid a decline." In the spirit of this definition, we focus our discussion on *opportunistic* earnings management by companies.

[39] To simplify exposition for the rest of the chapter, we will limit our discussion to fair value write-ups for holding gains. Our discussion implicitly includes consideration of holding losses associated with fair value write-downs.

Accounting Standards (SFAS) No. 115, *Accounting for Certain Investments in Debt and Equity Securities,* the holding gains on these securities temporarily bypass the income statement and are recorded as a direct increase in owners' equity. Only when these securities are sold can a company report the previously accumulated gains as part of its net income.[40] Thus, a company that expected to report lower-than-expected operating income could boost net income by selling some of its appreciated available-for-sale securities. These one-time gains can be difficult to identify because companies tend to group them with other miscellaneous income and expense items in the income statement. For example, the 1996 annual report for Dell Computer Corporation includes a line item on the face of the income statement called "Financing and other income (expense), net." A bit of digging in the footnotes reveals that realized marketable securities gains are included in this income statement account. Although no evidence suggests that Dell used these securities for the purpose of earnings management in its 1996 annual report, numerous examples exist of other companies selling winning securities to bolster net income. Such "cherry picking" has been extensively discussed in the business press (for example, see Staubus 1992 and Wechsler Linden 1990).

As summarized in **Exhibit 4,** *three* versions of case materials were included in the initial experiment.[41] A critically important feature of our experiment is that all of the information contained in the three versions was identical, except for the *amount* and *source* of earnings growth reported by the company. The NEM (no earnings management) company included financial information for an industrial company that previously wrote up its available-for-sale marketable securities for holding gains and simply continued to hold these securities. Consistent with SFAS No. 115, the holding gains on these securities were recorded as a nonretained earnings increase in owners' equity. Because the NEM firm did not sell the appreciated marketable securities, the holding gains were not realized and did not affect net income. Without realizing these gains in earnings, the NEM firm reported *no* growth in net income during the three years included in the case.

---

[40]Prior to the issuance of new comprehensive income disclosure requirements, analyzing the changes in unrealized holding gains and losses involved considerable detective work. A recent analysis conducted by Smith and Reither (1996) suggests that the fair value adjustment account balance was difficult to find in annual reports because companies often net it with other equity accounts. SFAS No. 130 requires explicit disclosure of activities in this arena.

[41]Although three versions of the case materials are described in this section, it is important to note that the analysts who participated in our study saw only *one* version of the materials. This type of experimental design—called "between subjects"—allows strong inferences about the cause of any observed differences between analysts' stock-price predictions.

 ©2000, The Research Foundation of AIMR

Exhibit 4. Description of Three Earnings Management Scenarios Included in the Field Experiment

Scenario	Description
No Earnings Management (NEM)	This case provided financial information for a hypothetical company for which reported net income was positive but included *zero growth* during the previous three years. The company's available-for-sale marketable securities portfolio included significant holding gains, but these gains cannot be recognized in reported net income until the marketable securities are sold.
Earnings Management (EM)	This case provided financial information for a hypothetical company for which reported net income was positive and included *11 percent growth* during the previous three years. This company is identical to the one in the NEM case, except for one important feature. The EM company achieved the 11 percent growth in reported net income by selling (and subsequently repurchasing) available-for-sale securities for which the company had holding gains. Because the company is an industrial firm, the realized holding gains included in reported net income should not be considered a persistent source of future earnings.
Increased Revenues (IR)	This case provided financial information for a hypothetical company for which reported net income was positive and included *11 percent growth* during the previous three years. This company is identical to that included in the EM case, except for one important feature. The IR company achieved its earnings growth through increased sales and *not* through sales of its marketable securities. Because the company is an industrial firm, the increase in revenues in the IR case should be considered a more persistent source of future earnings than the realized gains included in the EM case.

The second set of materials included financial information for a company that was identical to the NEM firm in all respects but one. The EM (earnings management) company previously wrote up its available-for-sale marketable securities for the same amount of holding gains as the NEM firm but strategically timed the sale of the securities over the next three years to realize the holding gains. In addition, the EM firm repurchased a similar amount of marketable securities immediately after the sales. This decision caused the firm to report 11 percent growth in net income during the three years included in the case. Again, an important feature of this study is that the EM firm is economically identical to the NEM firm. That is, even though the EM firm reported 11 percent growth in net income and the NEM firm reported no growth in net income, both firms experienced identical holding gains on their marketable securities and the book and market values of their current portfolios of marketable securities were identical. The only difference is that the EM firm's act of selling the appreciated securities and repurchasing similar securities shifts the holding gain from an accumulation account in owners' equity to net income and, ultimately, retained earnings.[42]

Comparison of analysts' valuation of the EM and NEM companies is interesting because the economically equivalent companies should have identical potential for persistent future abnormal earnings. However, if the EM company's earnings management is not adjusted for, analysts may believe its future earnings will be higher and assess a higher stock price to it than to the NEM firm. By itself, higher stock prices provided in the EM case do not necessarily indicate that analysts misinterpreted the persistence of earnings. Because comparing the EM and NEM cases to a third case in which the increase in earnings is from core productive activities would establish an upper bound for the appropriate valuation of the company, we created a third case (denoted IR—increased revenues) in which the company reported the same 11 percent annual growth in net income as the EM firm (hence, the same pattern of net income as the EM firm). In this case, however, the growth in earnings was caused by an increase in core revenues, instead of transitory gains from sales of marketable securities.

For a typical industrial or technology company, an increase in core revenues is a more persistent source of earnings than transitory gains recognized through the sale of marketable securities. Accordingly, in this experiment, the growth in earnings included in the IR case should provide a better indicator of future earnings. If the historical earnings figure is used directly in valuation, the IR case also should be assigned a higher multiple in valuation. The IR case thus provides a baseline against which to evaluate whether analysts detected the EM firm's earnings management. **Table 5** shows the most recent year of income statement and balance sheet information provided to analysts in the three versions of the materials. Again, each version of the case contained three years of comparative financial statements, each analyst only received one of these versions of the case, and analysts were not informed of the existence of the other versions of the case.

The materials in the study consisted of two parts, a stock-price valuation task and postexperiment questions. The company-specific information in the case was for a hypothetical company in the electronic measurement and

---

[42]Both firms recorded deferred taxes in the period the holding gain was experienced. Although a "real" tax payable is accrued in the period that the securities are actually sold, the amount of deferred taxes at the NEM firm and the sum of the remaining deferred taxes and the taxes payable at the EM firm are identical.

Table 5. Income Statement and Balance Sheet Information for the Three Earnings Management Scenarios Included in the Field Experiment

Item	NEM Materials	EM Materials	IR Materials
Most recent year of income statement information			
Revenues			
Sales of goods	$181,630	$181,630	$184,650
Costs and expenses			
Cost of goods sold	101,195	101,195	101,195
Selling, general, and administrative expenses	38,142	38,142	38,142
Research and development	18,890	18,890	18,890
Interest and other financing costs, net	11,006	7,986	11,006
Total costs and expenses	$169,233	$166,213	$169,233
Earnings from continuing operations before tax	12,397	15,417	15,417
Provision for income taxes	4,351	5,411	5,411
Net income	$8,046	$10,006	$10,006
Earnings per share	$0.81	$1.00	$1.00
Average number of shares outstanding	9,985	9,985	9,985
Most recent year of balance sheet information			
Current assets	$32,697	$32,697	$32,697
Cash	138,551	138,551	138,551
Available-for-sale securities	47,362	47,362	47,362
Accounts receivable, net	41,371	41,371	41,371
Inventory	259,981	259,981	259,981
Property, plant, and equipment, net	61,479	61,479	61,479
Other noncurrent assets	32,266	32,266	32,266
Total assets	$353,726	$353,726	$353,726
Liabilities			
Accounts payable and other current liabilities	90,178	90,178	90,178
Long-term notes payable	97,576	97,576	97,576
Other noncurrent liabilities	47,109	47,109	47,109
Total liabilities	$234,863	$234,863	$234,863
Stockholders' equity			
Common stock, at par	1,997	1,997	1,997
Additional paid-in capital	71,948	71,948	71,948
Retained earnings	36,600	39,794	36,600
Net unrealized gains on available-for-sale investments	8,318	5,124	8,318
Total stockholders' equity	$118,863	$118,863	$118,863
Total liabilities and stockholders' equity	$353,726	$353,726	$353,726

testing instruments industry (Standard Industrial Code 3825). This information was based on an actual company listed on the American Stock Exchange. We selected the industry and company through a search of the 1995 Compustat P/S/T database. In particular, we searched for companies that experienced a significant increase in the balance of unrealized gains and losses—relative to net income—in marketable equity securities (Compustat data item 238).[43] We obtained the company's financial statements via LEXIS-NEXIS and modified them to create the three versions of case materials.

Forty-seven buy-side equity analysts and portfolio managers participated in the study.[44] On average, the analysts had 14 years of experience as financial analysts (85 percent held the CFA designation) and spent an average of 40 percent of their time on equity security analysis and another 47 percent on portfolio management. In addition, on average, these analysts followed 52 companies (with a median of 40). The average size of the portfolio under their direct management was $810 million (median, $150 million) and their employers had $16 billion (median, $1.5 billion) of assets under management.

Participating analysts were provided with background information about the company, its industry, industry average P/Es and ranges, and summary historical financial information.[45] Participants also received a stylized press release (as disseminated by Bloomberg Financial Services) reporting the company's annual earnings. The press release also included the current year's financial statements and a summary of significant accounting policies. After reviewing the background information and the company's financial statements, as included in the press release, participants were asked to provide an estimate of the value of the company's common stock. Analysts also were asked to provide a written description of the manner in which they determined the stock price. After answering these questions, participants responded to a series of questions about the financial information in the case and several questions designed to determine whether analysts were aware of

---

[43]A significant increase in this item number suggests a high level of available-for-sale marketable securities holding gains relative to net income.

[44]All analysts were individually recruited from the *1996 Membership Directory* (AIMR 1997) on the basis of their self-reported job descriptions. After securing their agreement to participate, we distributed the materials via overnight mail to 65 analysts, yielding a 72 percent response rate. Sixty-two additional equity analysts and portfolio managers participated in a follow-up study on the usefulness of the FASB's new comprehensive income reporting requirement (see Hirst and Hopkins 1998). We discuss the follow-up study in the last section of this chapter.

[45]The P/E data were provided to indicate a reasonable range within which the company's stock price might fall. An actual stock price was not provided in the materials because, as discussed in Chapter 1, the results of Ball and Brown (1968) suggest that most information in net income is impounded into a company's stock price by the earnings release date.

the hypothetical company's manipulation of earnings. They also provided demographic information.

Analysis of Stock-Price Estimates

Because we designed the case materials so that the financial position (i.e., balance sheet) and cash flows of the companies in each case were equivalent, any differences in analysts' stock-price assessments reflect the extent to which historical net income is used in valuation. In particular, the only difference between the three cases was the level of growth (zero versus 11 percent) and the source (marketable securities gains versus core revenues) of net income growth for the company to be valued. The average price provided by each analyst for each of the three cases is presented in the first column of **Table 6**. A comparison between analysts' stock-price judgments for the cases gives an indication of the importance of reported net income in analysts' valuation activities.

The average price provided by analysts for both 11 percent growth cases (i.e., EM and IR) is $16.02. The average price provided by analysts in the case with zero percent growth (i.e., NEM) is $11.25. A t-test comparing these prices (EM and IR versus NEM) is highly significant ($t = 4.47$; $p = 0.0001$) and indicates that analysts in the two 11 percent growth cases provided much

Table 6.   Results of Field Experiment

	Dependent Variable		
Version of Case Materials	Analysts' Stock-Price Judgments	Analysts' Assessment of the Company's Reporting Quality	Analysts' Assessment of the Company's Potential for Growth in Future Net Income
IR			
Average score	$16.31	9.64	7.66
Standard deviation of scores	3.95	1.99	2.77
Number of responses	13	12	12
EM			
Average score	$15.78	8.66	8.63
Standard deviation of scores	2.99	2.07	2.42
Number of responses	16	15	16
NEM			
Average score	$11.25	9.14	6.37
Standard deviation of scores	3.80	1.87	2.70
Number of responses	18	16	18

higher average stock prices than analysts in the zero percent growth case. Because the main difference in information between the three cases is the level of net income reported by the company, this result provides compelling evidence that analysts used reported net income as a significant input into their valuation activities. Of course, one could make the argument that the higher reported net income in the 11 percent growth cases merely is an indicator of a company that is economically superior to the company in the zero percent growth case. If this argument is true, analysts may not be explicitly impounding historical earnings into price but rather may be reflecting the superior underlying fundamentals of the companies that also have higher growth in net income. We incorporated earnings management into our experiment to directly address this possibility and to reveal more fully the extent to which reported net income is used in valuation.

Comparing the prices provided by analysts in only the EM and NEM cases highlights the importance of historical reported net income in equity valuation. Comparison is helpful because the companies in the EM and NEM cases are economically identical except for one key difference: The EM company sold appreciated available-for-sale marketable equity securities and repurchased an identical amount, whereas the NEM firm simply continued to hold the securities. Elementary logic suggests that because the EM and NEM companies are economically equivalent, analysts' use of the different levels of reported net income in valuation is the cause of any observed differences in price judgments. As indicated in the first column of Table 6, the average price in the EM case was $15.78 and the average price in the NEM case was $11.25. A t-test comparing these prices is highly significant ($t = 4.53$; $p = 0.0006$) and indicates that analysts in the EM case valued the company significantly higher than analysts in the NEM case.

Comparison of the IR case to the EM case provides an indication of the extent to which analysts explicitly considered the marketable securities-based earnings management included in the EM case. The average price in the IR case was $16.31, and the average price in the NEM case was $15.78. A t-test comparing these prices is not significant ($t = 0.40$; $p = 0.694$) and suggests that analysts valued the 11 percent net income growth caused by an increase in core operating revenues similarly to the 11 percent net income growth caused by marketable securities sales. This finding suggests that bottom-line historical net income is a significant input into buy-side analysts' valuation judgments.[46]

---

[46]Nonetheless, some readers will be disturbed by the analysts' failure to distinguish between earnings based on growth in sales versus earnings based on strategic security sales. We return to that issue in our discussion of a follow-up study later in the chapter.

    ©2000, The Research Foundation of AIMR

After analysts provided their stock-price estimates, they rated various attributes of the company's financial data based on a 15-point scale. We asked for these ratings so that we could better understand *why* analysts estimated stock prices in the pattern observed for the three versions of the case. In addition, these ratings can help eliminate other, potentially confounding explanations for the experiment's stock-price results. For example, one explanation for the pattern of analysts' stock-price judgments is that they believed that the companies across the three versions of the case had different levels of financial reporting quality. To investigate this possibility, we asked analysts to provide ratings for four different items that were designed to provide an indication of the company's financial reporting quality. Specifically, analysts rated the quality of the company's reported net income (from very low to very high), the clarity of the company's financial statements (from not at all clear to very clear), the reliability of the company's financial statements (from very unreliable to very reliable) and the manner in which the financial statements portrayed the company's overall long-term financial performance (from very misleading to very truthful).

Because these questions were designed to measure the same underlying characteristic of the company, we constructed a composite measure of perceived reporting quality by taking a simple average of the four measures.[47] As reported in the second column of Table 6, the average perceived reporting quality rating was 9.64 in the IR condition, 8.66 in the EM condition, and 9.14 in the NEM condition. An *F*-test conducted on these means indicates that the perceived reporting quality did not differ between the three versions of the case ($F < 0.5$). This result suggests that analysts perceived financial reporting quality to be similar for all three cases and that the observed differences in stock-price judgments were caused by the variation in the levels of reported net income and not differences in analysts' perceptions of the company's reporting quality.

Another factor that could have contributed to the differences between analysts' common stock-price judgments is variation in the perceived growth potential for the company.[48] To gather information on this factor, we asked

---

[47] A Cronbach coefficient alpha score of 0.78 provides evidence that analysts' responses to these items are highly correlated and suggests that the four questions are measuring the same underlying characteristic.

[48] After providing their stock-price judgments, analysts were asked to provide a brief explanation of how they arrived at their price. Analysis of these explanations suggests that many analysts used an earnings-based multiple (e.g., P/E). Of course, an important determinant of the relationship between price and earnings is analysts' assessment of a company's prospects for earnings growth.

analysts to rate, on a 15-point scale (from very low to very high), the company's potential for future earnings growth. As summarized in the third column of Table 6, analysts who completed the EM case provided a mean rating for the company of 8.63 and believed the company had significantly better prospects for future earnings growth than analysts who completed the NEM case, with a mean rating of 6.37 ($t = 2.51$; $p = 0.016$). In contrast, analysts perceived no statistically significant difference ($t < 1$) between the IR case, with a mean rating of 7.66, and the EM case, with a mean rating of 8.63. These results suggest that management's opportunistic earnings management in the EM case was successful in making analysts believe the company's future prospects for earnings growth were better than for the NEM firm, even though the EM and NEM companies were economically identical. In addition, the opportunistic management of earnings in the EM case caused analysts to perceive the company's future prospects for earnings growth to be the same as that observed for the company that created the earnings growth through an increase in operating revenues (i.e., the IR company).

Insights from the Experiment

The results of this experiment suggest that buy-side financial analysts rely extensively on reported net income in performing equity security valuation. In particular, analysis of analysts' stock-price judgments and written explanations for those judgments suggest that buy-side analysts do not derive primary estimates of value from cash flow or balance sheet information.

The apparent importance of earnings in valuation presents both good news and cause for concern. First, the good news: Analysts' use of reported net income in valuation suggests that they appear to be comfortable with using earnings in valuation and may benefit from more careful consideration of issues related to earnings quality. As we argued in Chapter 2, rigorous earnings-based models (such as the discounted abnormal earnings model) present an opportunity for analysts to focus on a company's productive activities and competitive environment without becoming distracted by specific forecasts of cash flows. Although forecasted earnings are a critical input for pragmatic applications of the free cash flow model, the importance of this forecast often gets overshadowed by other items that affect the implementation of the model, such as concerns over which noncash items to back out of forecasted earnings to arrive at forecasted free cash flow and whether free cash flows are being reinvested in zero-NPV (net present value) projects. By remaining focused on estimating the persistent earnings of the company, analysts can eliminate layers of complexity that add little value to valuation activities.

Of course, to appropriately apply a discounted abnormal earnings (DAE) model—or any valuation model for that matter—analysts must carefully consider the model's inputs. In particular, analysts should pay special attention to the underlying quality of historical reported earnings, if this number is being used to forecast future earnings. The need to forecast future earnings in the DAE model leads to a potentially troubling result for this experiment: Companies may be able to engage in opportunistic earnings management and may be able to do so without being detected by many analysts.[49]

How might analysts avoid the valuation pitfalls presented by firms that opportunistically manage their earnings? This question is not easy to answer because financial statement analysis is a difficult and time-consuming task that rarely leads to a single, clear, all-encompassing conclusion about a company. In addition, as reported in this chapter, analysts who participated in our experiment follow, on average, 52 companies and split their time between analysis and portfolio management. Given the demands on their time, the many ways in which companies can manage their earnings, and the complexity of financial information, analysts cannot realistically be expected to detect every instance of opportunistic earnings management. Analysts might be more likely to detect the sort of earnings management engaged in by the EM firm if they are provided with clearer disclosure of activity in marketable securities. We tested this possibility in a follow-up study.

Follow-Up Study

In Chapter 2, we noted that the FASB recently adopted a reporting standard for comprehensive income reporting. SFAS No. 130 was issued to facilitate the item-by-item assessment of companies' earnings performance. In particular, some proponents of the standard suggested that all performance-related changes in owners' equity should be presented in a single statement so that analysts could determine the value relevance of each of the performance-related line items. Indeed, in the context of our experiment, explicit reconciliation of marketable securities gains and losses in a performance statement might have helped analysts detect the opportunistic earnings management in

---

[49]Skeptics might argue that our findings would not hold in "real life" because participating analysts did not have the proper incentives to take the task seriously. We contend that this argument is incorrect for three reasons. First, participants were individually contacted and agreed to participate in the study. They were aware that the researchers could identify their responses and, therefore, likely felt a high degree of accountability. Second, the models they said they used to arrive at the valuations were the same ones they said they use on an everyday basis. Finally, the time they devoted to the task is not unrepresentative of the average time they would have to devote to an individual holding in their portfolios. These facts suggest that the data are reliable and likely to hold in natural settings.

the EM case. Accordingly, we performed a follow-up study to investigate the possibility that the new reporting standard for comprehensive income increases the likelihood that analysts will detect opportunistic earnings management through examination of the marketable securities portfolio and adjust their valuation judgments accordingly.

An interesting feature of SFAS No. 130 is that it does not require a specific format or location for the reporting of comprehensive income. Indeed, the only hard and fast requirement of the new standard is that companies disclose comprehensive income information in one of the primary financial statements. Although the FASB expressed a preference for reporting comprehensive income in a separate performance statement (consistent with their original exposure draft of the standard), most companies report comprehensive income in the statement of changes in equity (SCE). Because analysts currently regard the SCE as one of the least useful sources of financial information (Brown 1997), it is possible that SCE reporting of comprehensive income and its components will be less useful than reporting the same information in a separate performance report.

To address the potential benefit of the new comprehensive income information, we investigated whether a separate performance statement format and the SCE format, which is more likely to be used by most companies, are equally likely to correct the bias in analysts' stock-price judgments in the EM case.[50] We generated four additional experimental conditions (that is, in addition to the original EM and NEM conditions reported in Table 6, in which comprehensive income was not disclosed but could be derived from the financial statements). For each firm, we created two conditions in which a reconciliation of net income and comprehensive income was provided, as shown in **Table 7**. In one condition, the reconciliation was provided in a separate statement of performance immediately after the income statement. In the other condition, the reconciliation was included in the statement of changes in equity. In total, we analyzed six conditions: earnings management with no reconciliation of net income and comprehensive income (EM-No-CI); no earnings management with no reconciliation of net income and comprehensive income (NEM-No-CI); earnings management with the reconciliation included in SCE (EM-CI-SCE); no earnings management with reconciliation included in SCE (NEM-CI-SCE); earnings management with reconciliation provided in a separate statement immediately after the income statement (EM-CI-IS); and no earnings management with reconciliation provided in a separate statement immediately after the income statement (NEM-CI-IS). In

---

[50]This research was originally published in Hirst and Hopkins (1998).

©2000, The Research Foundation of AIMR

Table 7. Reconciliation of Net Income and Comprehensive Income in the CI-IS Conditions of Follow-Up Study

Comprehensive Income Disclosure	EM-CI-IS Condition	NEM-CI-IS Condition
Net income	$10,006	$8,046
Other comprehensive income		
Unrealized gains on available-for-sale securities arising this period		
Gross unrealized gain	1,379	1,379
Income tax	(484)	(484)
Net unrealized gain	895	895
Reclassification adjustment for realized gains on available-for-sale securities included in net income		
Gross realized gain	(3,020)	0
Income tax	1,060	0
Net realized gain	(1,960)	0
Total other comprehensive income	($1,065)	$895
Comprehensive income	$8,941	$8,941

Note: Data from Hirst and Hopkins (1998).

total, 96 buy-side analysts participated in the study—34 from the initial No-CI conditions and 62 additional analysts for the CI-SCE and CI-IS conditions.

We predicted that the clear disclosure of elements of other comprehensive income in the EM-CI-IS condition would lead analysts to detect the earnings management and to reach the same valuation for both the EM and NEM companies. Given that the disclosure of elements of other comprehensive income in the EM-CI-SCE condition is not as clear as in the EM-CI-IS condition but is clearer than in the EM-No CI condition, we did not make a specific prediction about whether that disclosure format would be effective in allowing analysts to detect earnings management and reach an appropriate valuation for the company.

As expected, within the study, clear reporting of comprehensive income and its components in a separate performance statement (i.e., the CI-IS conditions) helped analysts recognize the opportunistic earnings management in the EM case and led them to reach approximately the same judgment about stock price as did analysts completing the NEM case. Analysts provided a mean stock price for the EM-CI-IS condition of $13.40 versus $12.57 for the NEM-CI-IS condition. The difference between the average prices is not statistically significant, with a t-statistic of 0.66. This finding suggests that when analysts recognized that opportunistic earnings management was causing the smooth earnings growth of 11 percent (in the EM case), they adjusted their valuation judgments to reflect it. Interestingly, reporting comprehensive income and its components in the SCE did not mitigate the difference in stock-price judgments between the EM and NEM cases. Analysts provided a mean stock price of $14.81 for the EM-CI-SCE condition versus $12.49 for the NEM-CI-SCE condition ($t = 1.85$; $p = 0.034$).

The finding that comprehensive income disclosures have more impact when disclosed in a separate statement of performance than in the SCE is consistent with the survey data reported in Brown (1997). In particular, Brown reports that analysts regard the SCE as one of the least useful reports provided by companies. In our study, analysts apparently disregarded the potentially important value-relevant information in the SCE. One reason that analysts might ignore the SCE is that prior to the issuance of the reporting standard for comprehensive income, although the major transactions reported in the SCE and not in other statements (i.e., stock issuances and buybacks, dividends) were highly significant, analysts were likely to have known such information before the release of the financial statements. With useful disclosures becoming more likely to appear in the SCE, analysts may begin to pay more attention to that statement. The findings of the follow-up study suggest that ignoring the SCE may allow certain forms of earnings management to go undetected.

Summary

We conducted two studies to evaluate how buy-side analysts use earnings information in their valuation process. The findings of the initial study, which indicated that analysts have trouble detecting opportunistic earnings management, suggest that analysts need to pay more attention to the sources of earnings and not simply focus on the amount. The separate follow-up study tested whether different ways of reporting comprehensive income and its components might mitigate analysts' inability to detect opportunistic earnings management. The findings of this experiment support the view that clear disclosure of all performance-related items would allow analysts to more easily incorporate value relevant information into their valuations.

©2000, The Research Foundation of AIMR

Chapter 4. Conclusion

This research project began with the goal of providing analysts with the answer to the question "What are earnings?" One might think that answering this question would be fairly straightforward for two accounting professors. As we considered ways to formulate our answer, however, we quickly realized how big this question actually is. In the United States, academic accounting scholars have spent the better part of the 20th century trying to answer this question, and this quest has generated some wonderful insights about the definition and measurement of "true" economic earnings—from the academic's philosophical perspective. Little of this research, however, could directly benefit a practicing equity analyst in answering our initial question. Because equity analysts are, first and foremost, concerned with valuation, our primary goal in writing this monograph was to demystify reported earnings and to explain how they can best be incorporated into valuation activities.

In Chapter 1, we provided selected highlights from the large body of academic research that demonstrate the relevance of accounting information to security prices. This body of research documents the importance not only of the bottom-line net income figure but also of components of earnings. If the goal is to forecast future free cash flows, current accounting earnings actually are more helpful than current-period cash flows. The bulk of prior research, however, addresses the relation between accounting data and aggregate, market-level data, such as stock prices and returns, and little research has investigated the valuation judgments and decision making of individual analysts.

As with any other model, the output of an earnings-based valuation model will only be as good as its inputs. To help improve the quality of accounting inputs in the valuation process, Chapter 2 outlined the way accountants classify components of earnings and provided examples of how these classifications help analysts determine the quality and persistence of historical earnings. To help analysts see through the potential biases inherent in financial data provided by management, we emphasized the importance of understanding the discretion involved in making accounting classifications. Being armed with better knowledge about how accounting data are generated puts analysts in a better position to use the information effectively.

Chapter 3 describes two studies that investigate the valuation judgments of individual buy-side equity analysts. The initial study provides direct evidence that the level of a firm's accounting earnings influences professional buy-side analysts' valuation judgments. A troubling finding, however, is that the analysts did not appear to distinguish between firms that were and were not managing their earnings through the strategic timing of sales and repurchases of marketable securities.

We hypothesized that this result may have been a function of the way the accounting data were presented to the analysts. Although the efficient market hypothesis maintains that data presentation ought not affect security prices, we argued that given the nature of security analysts' jobs (i.e., the number of firms they follow and the other demands on their time), analysts may require clearer disclosure of such transactions if they are to incorporate such data into stock price judgments. In a follow-up study (Hirst and Hopkins 1998), we investigated this hypothesis and found that comprehensive income disclosures do indeed help analysts uncover earnings management. We provided evidence of the benefits to analysts of lobbying the Financial Accounting Standards Board for improvements in accounting standards and evidence to the FASB of the implications of their new comprehensive income standard.

Our hope is that analysts will benefit from better knowledge of what earnings are and how they can be incorporated into equity valuation. In addition, we hope that readers have gained an appreciation for the value of examining the judgments and decision making of individual analysts. In our view, continued research in this area can lead to insights about how analysts do their job, how expert and novice analysts differ, how to improve the education and training of analysts, and most important, how to improve the practice of equity analysis.

©2000, The Research Foundation of AIMR

References

Abelson, A. 1996. "Big Blue Sky." *Barron's* (January 22):3.

Anderson, M. 1988. "A Comparative Analysis of Information Search and Evaluation of Professional and Non-Professional Financial Analysts." *Accounting, Organizations and Society*, vol. 13, no. 5 (September):431–446.

Association for Investment Management and Research. 1993. *Financial Reporting in the 1990s and Beyond*. Charlottesville, VA: AIMR.

Association for Investment Management and Research. 1997. *1996 Membership Directory*. Charlottesville, VA: AIMR.

Ball, R., and P. Brown. 1968. "An Empirical Evaluation of Accounting Income Numbers." *Journal of Accounting Research*, vol. 6, no. 2 (Autumn):159–178.

Bank, D. 2000. "Microsoft Net Tops Estimates, Boosted by Portfolio Gains." *Wall Street Journal Interactive Edition* (January 19).

Bauman, M.P. 1996. "A Review of Fundamental Analysis Research in Accounting." *Journal of Accounting Literature*, vol. 15:1–33.

Beaver, W., R. Clarke, and W. Wright. 1979. "The Association between Unsystematic Securities Returns and the Magnitude of Earnings Forecast Errors." *Journal of Accounting Research*, vol. 17, no. 2 (Autumn):316–340.

Bernard, V.L. 1989. "Capital Markets Research in Accounting During the 1980s: A Critical Review." In *The State of Accounting Research as We Enter the 1990s*. Edited by T.J. Frecka. Urbana-Champaign, IL: University of Illinois.

———.1995. "The Feltham-Ohlson Framework: Implications for Empiricists." *Contemporary Accounting Research*, vol. 11, no. 2 (Spring):733–748.

Brealey, R.A., and S.C. Myers. 1991. *Principles of Corporate Finance*. 4th ed. New York: McGraw-Hill, Inc.

Brennan, M.J. 1995. "A Perspective on Accounting and Stock Prices." *Journal of Applied Corporate Finance*, vol. 8, no. 1 (Spring):43–50.

Bricker, R., G. Previts, T. Robinson, and S. Young. 1995. "Financial Analyst Assessment of Company Earnings Quality." *Journal of Accounting, Auditing and Finance*, vol. 10, no. 3 (Summer):541–554.

Brown, P.R. 1997. "Financial Data and Decision Making by Sell-Side Analysts." *Journal of Financial Statement Analysis*, vol. 2, no. 3 (Spring):43–49.

Cheng, C.S.A., C.S. Liu, and T.F. Schaefer. 1996. "Earnings Permanence and the Incremental Information Content of Cash Flows from Operations." *Journal of Accounting Research*, vol. 34, no. 1 (Spring):173–181.

Chipello, C.J. 1998. "MacMillan Bloedel to Sell Paper Unit for $593.6 Million." *Wall Street Journal* (April 24):A6.

Cho, Y.J., and K. Jung. 1991. "Earnings Response Coefficients: A Synthesis of Theory and Empirical Evidence." *Journal of Accounting Literature*, vol. 10:85–116.

Collins, D.W., E.L. Maydew, and I.S. Weiss. 1997. "Changes in the Value-Relevance of Earnings and Book Values over the Past Forty Years." *Journal of Accounting and Economics*, vol. 24, no. 1 (December): 39–67.

Copeland, T., T. Koller, and J. Murrin. 1996. *Valuation: Measuring and Managing the Value of Companies*. 2nd ed. New York: John Wiley & Sons, Inc.

Dechow, P.M. 1994. "Accounting Earnings and Cash Flows as Measures of Firm Performance: The Role of Accounting Accruals." *Journal of Accounting and Economics*, vol. 18, no. 1 (July):3–42.

Easton, P.D., T.S. Harris, and J.A. Ohlson. 1992. "Aggregate Accounting Earnings Can Explain Most of Security Returns." *Journal of Accounting and Economics*, vol. 15, no. 2/3 (June/September):119–142.

Edwards, E.O., and P.W. Bell. 1961. *The Theory and Measurement of Business Income*. Berkeley, CA: University of California Press.

Elliott, J.A., and J.D. Hanna. 1996. "Repeated Accounting Write-Offs and the Information Content of Earnings." *Journal of Accounting Research*, vol. 34 (Supplement):135–156.

Feltham, G.A., and J.A. Ohlson. 1995. "Valuation and Clean Surplus Accounting for Operating and Financial Activities." *Contemporary Accounting Research*, vol. 11, no. 2 (Spring):689–731.

Francis, J., P. Olsson, and D.R. Oswald. 2000. "Comparing the Accuracy and Explainability of Dividend, Free Cash Flow and Abnormal Earnings Equity Value Estimates." *Journal of Accounting Research*, vol. 38, no. 1 (Spring):135–156.

Frank, S.E., and E.S. Browning. 1998. "Assortment of One-Time Gains Help Boost Citicorp's Earnings." *Wall Street Journal* (January 28):C1.

Goldman, Sachs & Company. 1997. *EVA: A Primer.* (September 10).

Hand, J.R.M. 1989. "Did Firms Undertake Debt-Equity Swaps for an Accounting Paper Profit or True Financial Gain?" *Accounting Review*, vol. 64, no. 4 (October):587–623.

Hirst, D.E., and P.E. Hopkins. 1998. "Comprehensive Income Reporting and Analysts' Valuation Judgments." *Journal of Accounting Research*, vol. 36 (Supplement):47–75.

Kormendi, R., and R. Lipe. 1987. "Earnings Innovations, Earnings Persistence, and Stock Returns. *Journal of Business*, vol. 60, no. 3 (July):323–346.

Laing, J.R. 1998. "Dangerous Games." *Barron's Online* (June 8).

Lev, B. 1989. "On the Usefulness of Earnings and Earnings Research: Lessons and Directions from Two Decades of Empirical Research." *Journal of Accounting Research*, vol. 27 (Supplement):153–192.

Lev, B., and J.A. Ohlson. 1982. "Market-Based Empirical Research in Accounting: A Review, Interpretation, and Extension." *Journal of Accounting Research*, vol. 20 (Supplement):249–322.

Lowenstein, R. 1997. "Stocks Worth Writing Off." *Smart Money*, vol. 6, no. 12 (December):67–70.

Mear, R., and M. Firth. 1987. "Cue Usage and Self-Insight of Financial Analysts." *Accounting Review*, vol. 62, no. 1 (January):176–182.

———.1990. "A Parsimonious Description of Individual Differences in Financial Analyst Judgment." *Journal of Accounting, Auditing and Finance*, vol. 5, no. 4 (Fall):501–526.

Ohlson, J.A. 1995. "Earnings, Book Values, and Dividends in Equity Valuation." *Contemporary Accounting Research*, vol. 11, no. 2 (Spring):661–687.

Palepu, K.G., V.L. Bernard, and P.M. Healy. 1996. *Business Analysis & Valuation Using Financial Statements.* Cincinnati, OH: South-Western College Publishing.

Penman, S.H. 1992. "Return to Fundamentals." *Journal of Accounting, Auditing and Finance*, vol. 7, no. 4 (Fall):465–483.

Penman, S.H., and T. Sougiannis. 1998. "A Comparison of Dividend, Cash Flow, and Earnings Approaches to Equity Valuation." *Contemporary Accounting Research*, vol. 15, no. 3 (Fall):343–383.

Preinreich, G.A.D. 1938. "Annual Survey of Economic Theory: The Theory of Depreciation." *Econometrica*, vol. 6, no. 3 (July):219–241.

Previts, G.J., R.J. Bricker, T.R. Robinson, and S.J. Young. 1994. "A Content Analysis of Sell-Side Financial Analyst Company Reports." *Accounting Horizons*, vol. 8, no. 2 (June):55–70.

Rappaport, A. 1998. "Three Ways Stock-Market Investors Can Stack the Odds in Their Favor." *Wall Street Journal* (February 26):R6.

Schrand, C.M., and B.R. Walther. 2000. "Strategic Benchmarks in Earnings Announcements: The Selective Disclosure of Prior-Period Earnings Components." *Accounting Review,* vol. 75, no. 2 (April):151-177.

Serwer, A. 1998. "Street Life." *Fortune.com* (July 1).

Sloan, R.G. 1996. "Using Earnings and Free Cash Flow to Evaluate Corporate Performance." *Bank of America Journal of Applied Corporate Finance*, vol. 9, no. 1 (Spring):70–78.

Smith, P.A., and C.L. Reither. 1996. "Comprehensive Income and the Effect of Reporting It." *Financial Analysts Journal*, vol. 52, no. 6 (November/December):14–19.

Smith, R., and S. Lipin. 1996. "Odd Numbers: Are Companies Using Restructuring Costs To Fudge the Figures?" *Wall Street Journal* (January 30):A1.

Smith, R., S. Lipin, and A.K. Naj. 1994. "Managing Profits: How General Electric Damps Fluctuations in Its Annual Earnings." *Wall Street Journal* (November 3):A1.

Staubus, G.J. 1992. "Cherry Pickers' Friend." *Barron's* (December 7):16–17.

Wechsler Linden, D. 1990. "If Life Is Volatile, Account For It." *Forbes* (November 12):114.

White, G.I., A.C. Sondhi, and D. Fried. 1998. *The Analysis and Use of Financial Statements*. 2nd ed. New York: John Wiley & Sons, Inc.

Selected AIMR Publications

AIMR Performance Presentation Standards Handbook, 2nd edition, 1997

Alternative Investing, 1998

Asian Equity Investing, 1998

Asset Allocation in a Changing World, 1998

Credit Analysis Around the World, 1998

Currency Risk in Investment Portfolios, 1999

Derivatives in Portfolio Management, 1998

Ethical Issues for Today's Firm, 2000

Equity Research and Valuation Techniques, 1998

Frontiers in Credit-Risk Analysis, 1999

The Future of Investment Management, 1998

Investment Counseling for Private Clients, 1999

Practical Issues in Equity Analysis, 2000

Risk Management: Principles and Practices, 1999

Standards of Practice Handbook, 8th edition, 1999

The Technology Industry: Impact of the Internet, 2000

A full catalog of publications is available on AIMR's World Wide Web site at **www.aimr.org**; or you may write to AIMR, P.O. Box 3668, Charlottesville, VA 22903 U.S.A.; call 1-804-951-5499; fax 1-804-951-5262; or e-mail **info@aimr.org** to receive a free copy. All prices are subject to change.